ACCIDENTAL BLOOMS

T0009255

Copyright © 2023 Keiko Honda

01 02 03 04 05 27 26 25 24 23

All rights reserved. No part of this publication may be reproduced, stored in a retrieval system or transmitted, in any form or by any means, without prior permission of the publisher or, in the case of photocopying or other reprographic copying, a licence from Access Copyright, the Canadian Copyright Licensing Agency, www.accesscopyright.ca, 1-800-893-5777, info@accesscopyright.ca.

Caitlin Press Inc.
3375 Ponderosa Way
Qualicum Beach, BC V9K 2J8
www.caitlinpress.com

Text and cover design by Vici Johnstone
Artwork by Keiko Honda
Edited by Holly Vestad
Printed in Canada

Caitlin Press Inc. acknowledges financial support from the Government of Canada and the Canada Council for the Arts, and the Province of British Columbia through the British Columbia Arts Council and the Book Publisher's Tax Credit.

Library and Archives Canada Cataloguing in Publication

Accidental blooms : a memoir / by Keiko Honda.
Honda, Keiko (Artist), author.
Canadiana 20230205852 | ISBN 9781773861210 (softcover)
LCSH: Honda, Keiko (Artist) | LCSH: Artists—British Columbia—Biography. | LCSH:
    Autoimmune diseases—Patients—British Columbia—Biography. | CSH: Japanese Canadians—British
    Columbia—Biography. | LCGFT: Autobiographies.
LCC N6549.H647 A2 2023 | DDC 700.92—dc23

ACCIDENTAL BLOOMS

A MEMOIR

BY KEIKO HONDA

Caitlin Press 2023

This book is dedicated to my loving and brilliant daughter, Maya.

*Your endearing smiles and sparkling eyes light up my life and beyond.
Keep smiling, sweetheart.*

CONTENTS

FOREWORD

As I write this in 2023, I am balancing on the edge—an artist with flaws. My watercolour paintings have many "blooms," unintentional, unpredictable eruptions of colour that beginners produce when pigment flows uninvited from one region to another across a too-wet surface. When I have an accidental bloom, I feel a camaraderie with it, because it calls to mind someone plunging over unfamiliar borders. Like many of us, I am trying to create (or find) an equilibrium, like pooling water or paint coming to rest.

My life has followed a series of sharp transformations, forced adaptations and unexpected kindness. Born and raised in Japan, I moved to the US with my Canadian husband, completed a PhD in community health science at New York University, then went into research. After finishing a postdoctoral fellowship in cancer epidemiology at Columbia University, I gave birth to my daughter, Maya, and then took up a research job at Columbia. I lived a busy life in Manhattan as mother, wife and research scientist. Then, without any warning or volition, that life ended—yet I never felt so strongly that my life mattered as I did then.

At Columbia, I was studying the role of social support networks in cancer prevention and control, and how these networks affect health and resilience. After my accident, I suddenly experienced these social support networks in the flesh, in a very personal kind of research. Unexpectedly, they were fluid and dynamic, like water pooling on a surface.

No longer hindered by academia or any market imperative, I could even reinvent myself. Soon, I was engaged in a different kind of research: running a series of artists' salons, preaching the virtues of artistic creation and, surprisingly, I converted myself by reflexive osmosis. I became able to exercise my freedom to live with change. Through writing and watercolours, I am re-rendering my life, understanding my Japanese childhood, my years in academia, maternity and other challenges anew through the richness of my own experience.

Co-creation, I have discovered, is the key to social support networks. These networks are not simply groups one joins, but ones we co-create by giving, connecting. The more we are supported, the more we can give, like aqueous nutrients cycling through an ecosystem. Humans are, by design, communal organisms. Healthy cultures understand that.

I am exploring my own role as an emerging artist, as I raise my daughter and run a non-profit that promotes cultural diversity and artistic self-discovery. Self-discovery through art fosters cultural resilience and social health. Accidental watercolour blooms may serve as symbols for how we can rethink our norms, blend social and disciplinary boundaries, and discover new ways to flower.

At its best, *making* becomes *finding*—finding meaning, finding a way of looking that connects all things. Within this process of finding, I hope to provoke conversations. In this sense, this book is meant to be a collaboration with my readers. I hope to enhance our awareness of previously unseen possibilities, the way watercolour blooms turn out to be accidently beautiful. Each chapter presents one or two artistic or philosophical ideas. They are always conversations.

Grandma Tamiko in her signature kappōgi (covered apron), a cherished sight from my childhood. *Where it All Began*, 2019

Prologue: Wellspring

Spring 1975

A sea of white blossoms churned in the wind. My grandmother's plum tree was, miraculously for this southern Japanese climate, still blooming in late March.

Zaki, zaki, zaki, zaki. Wrapped in a spotless, white-sleeved apron, Tamiko, my maternal grandmother, was scaling fish that my grandfather, Konosuke, caught earlier that day. *Zaki, zaki, zaki, zaki.* The two dozen bright red *kinmedai* were splashing in the cooler. Extended family living nearby were coming for dinner. As was our tradition, my youngest uncle was jumping into the car to pick up relatives living farther away so they could join us. All four gas burners were in full flame. Steam was hissing through the ill-fitted lid of the large soup pot, making rhythmic sounds in unison with the *zaki, zaki, zaki* of scaling fish like a percussion score. In his atelier, Konosuke was creating a fish print (called *gyotaku*) with Japanese *sumi* ink and paper to immortalize the other fish, a huge red sea bream, that he had also caught that morning. Like most men of his generation, he rarely entered a kitchen. I saw him from a distance, passing through the corridor as he approached us. Then: "Ba-chan (Grandma), a cup of tea please." He said it gently. He gave me a boyish smile and nodded to signal how he loved the smell of the cooking in progress. I had just turned seven years old.

As usual, to make *kinmedai* soup, grandmother would broil the fish until charred around the edges, garnish with *mitsuba* (a kind of Japanese parsley that she would handweave into loops as edible ornaments) and serve it in a delicate broth of wine and seaweed. I was taught to eat every piece of flesh, including the eyeballs. My mother often said eating these soft bits would make us smarter. I always ate them last because I was fascinated by the tiny, light-blue lenses hidden under the gelatin.

I was born in Kumamoto, in the southernmost region of Japan, where I spent my childhood and adolescence in an endless cycle of life with the many land and sea creatures that live there too. The city of Kumamoto is known as the Land of Water and has the best drinking water in Japan. It is pure, natural mineral water, very soft and tasty. The city relies on groundwater for most of the region's drinking water, supplying a population slightly larger than Vancouver's. Our ancestors erected many tiny shrines adjacent to the water source long ago, honouring the spirit that lives in the water. Locals keep the shrines intact and spread our ancestors' appreciation for water and all that nature gives us. Even today, Japanese spirituality is deeply rooted in this kind of animism, the concept that everything, living or non-living, has a spirit or a soul. My family raised me—but perhaps the Kumamoto water did too.

My father worked for the national telephone company and travelled often. My mother was a full-time nurse in a large hospital and frequently worked night shifts. A dual-income family was not typical back then, but my parents were not conventional. They designed and built a home near my grandparents. "Close enough to share a hot meal," as we always said. My parents needed help with childcare, but they also wanted us to have a close relationship with our grandparents. So, until the new home was finished when I was six, I lived with my maternal grandparents. I slept with my grandmother every night. I remember her telling us stories of mythical creatures as vividly as if she had seen them herself. Many relatives lived close by and we often got together to enjoy each other's company.

Zaki, zaki, zaki, zaki.

"Ba-chan, may I help you?" I asked.

"Thank you, Keiko-chan, but your beautiful whitefish-like hands will get spoiled. You can sip green tea and eat cherry blossom rice cake over there." She smiled. Every time she spoke to me or anyone on the street, she always used the very polite Japanese verb forms, as did my grandfather. I always felt loved and treasured.

"Ba-chan, I want to help. What can I do?" I insisted. She was now dressing the fish and making a criss-cross cut in its skin.

"Okay, I will teach you how to tie *mitsuba*." She grabbed two blanched *mitsuba* and tied them together into one loop. "*Mitsuba* is a good luck charm. You can join a few stems and make loops, like this," she continued, demonstrating. "For generations, Japanese people have wished for good bonds between people that will bring health and happiness." Her voice was so tender. Briefly, she had a distant look in her eyes.

"You will live to be one hundred, Ba-chan!" I exclaimed.

"Now you try, Keiko-chan." The blanched stems were flexible but slippery. I managed to make enough *mitsuba* loops for the whole family. The knot reminded me of *obijime*, decorative strings that hold a kimono sash. I had recently worn one for the celebration of my seventh year of life—a traditional Japanese ritual where children aged three, five and seven dress up in kimonos and go to a shrine to celebrate their growth.

Guests were arriving with food: wild vegetable rice, bamboo shoot salad, fried Spanish mackerel in *nanban* (sweet and sour) sauce. The aromas were seductive. I excitedly but carefully placed my looped *mitsuba* on the perfectly broiled fish. The intense green dramatically contrasted with the red flesh of the fish, and it bound together the space, taste and people.

"See, the fish is dressed in a kimono!" I exclaimed. The fish looked elegant and sacred.

At the crowded table, everyone was chatting, laughing and filling up each other's beer cups. *Gyotaku*, the print of the red sea bream Konosuke made, was signed, framed and hung up on the wall, while the fish itself was now before us on the table, transformed into sashimi.

"*Itadakimasu!*" we said in chorus.

Fishing a *mitsuba* loop out of my soup bowl, I proudly announced, "I made these!" and recited what I had just learned about how *mitsuba* symbolizes the deep bonds between people. In the future, the course of my life would test those bonds. I ate every piece of meat, two eyeballs and *mitsuba*—my new lucky charm.

My childhood was connected to water and everything that lived in it. As far back as I can remember, my playground consisted of rice paddies and the streams near my house. In spring and summer, I routinely discovered a world of wonder under the lush green carpet of the paddies. I would watch, spellbound, as millions of freshly hatched *medaka* swam between my bare feet in the muddy water. I learned in school that their ancient ancestors lived in the sea, so they could adapt to salt water quickly when the tide came in. The *medaka* had ancient bodily memories; what were mine?

Like a tiny *medaka*, I was raised in the lush and plentiful ecosystems of Kumamoto, drinking water infused with rich minerals from

Mount Aso and the Ariake Sea. My childhood was fortified with close family bonds and ample nature. I swam and kept swimming in the rapidly flowing rivers of change that inescapably drew me to the open sea. Would I be able to survive in salt water, like a *medaka*? Eventually, I would cross the wide Pacific Ocean and arrive in New York City—to the Japanese, the Wild West. Little did I know then what the city would give me, and what it would take from me.

THE MAELSTROM

December 11, 2006

It was a typical Monday morning in Manhattan, where I had been living for over a dozen years. I was sitting at the dining table, holding my coffee mug with my left hand and scrolling through my work emails on my laptop with my right. I was an associate research scientist in the department of epidemiology at Columbia University, where I had just emerged from a gruelling postdoctoral fellowship in cancer epidemiology. I had published over a dozen articles in peer-reviewed journals and I was driven by the mantra, "Publish or perish." People at Columbia were friendly but driven and independent. Now that I had a new academic appointment in the same department, the survival game was accelerating. I was also the mother of a twenty-month-old baby, and I had not a minute to spare. Maya was still sleeping in the next room after being breastfed just a little earlier. I was struggling with weaning as I felt breastfeeding was the ultimate gift for both mother and baby.

It was already 8 a.m. My husband, Dan, a Harvard-educated invest-ment banker on Wall Street for the previous twelve years, had just left for work. As a managing director, he had an exceptional ability to main-tain a work-life balance while handling multiple high-profile business dealings and confidential matters. We were both thirty-eight and had reached the foot of what seemed like the second mountain in our re-spective fields, and we were willing to endure tremendous pressure as we climbed.

I finished breakfast, nursed Maya again, put her down for another short nap and got back to work. Suddenly, I felt a slight numbness and tingling in my right hand and right leg at the same time. I had an intu-itive feeling that something was wrong. I stopped typing and focussed all my attention on my right hand and leg, hoping it was just a spasm. I had always been healthy, never smoked nor drank, exercised and swam regularly, maintained my ideal weight and had almost never been sick. The numbness and tingling did not disappear. *Uh oh*, I thought. I feared it was a transient ischemic attack as I had been sleeping poorly since becoming a mother. The three of us always slept in our king-sized bed together, with Maya in the middle so that I could nurse at night. I often woke up thirsty. Did I have poor blood flow to the brain? I started googling a neurologist in the city that I could see the next day.

By 10:30 a.m., I started noticing some changes. My right leg was starting to feel heavier and weaker. The numbness and tingling in my right hand and leg were still there. I called my parents in Japan, as I did regularly. My mom, a retired nurse, picked up the phone.

"I just sent you a Christmas present by express mail. Maya is growing so beautiful by the day, isn't she?" From her lively voice, I could picture her infectious smile. I did not have time for small talk, though, and broke the news cautiously.

"Mom, I might be having a minor stroke. Both my right hand and leg are numb and tingling. What do you think I should do?"

Immediately, she said, "Call Dan."

"I think he's in a meeting and I don't want to bother him unless it's an emergency." I did not realize how little time I had to make decisions and act.

"Okay, but please call me back and let me know if anything changes. And please call Dan."

"Yes, mom. Thank you," I said.

As soon as I hung up the phone, I stood up to walk to the next room to check on my napping baby—only I couldn't lift my right leg. My heart started pounding. Things were getting worse quickly and I realized I had little time. I ditched the plan to make an appointment with a neurologist and decided to rush to an emergency room (ER), but not by ambulance: when you call an ambulance, the paramedics have to bring you to the nearest hospital, with no exceptions. That means they would have brought me to a mid-sized hospital with no 24-7 magnetic resonance imaging (MRI) and few specialists on site. That could potentially mean delay in diagnosis and treatment. I knew I needed to go either uptown to Columbia Presbyterian or to New York University's (NYU) hospital, at the time called Tisch. *I have connections at Columbia... but NYU is closer to me... but crossing Manhattan at rush hour, with that heavy midtown traffic...* My mind was a mess.

As I was deciding I called two friends, one to take me to the hospital and one to stay with Maya. At the same time, I frantically started packing a bag with clothes, contact lens solutions, sanitary items, cosmetics (just in case) and my notebook and laptop. I knew I would be spending at least one night.

By this point, it was 11 a.m. and I was barely able to walk. My right leg was losing all its strength. Trying not to fall, I was dragging my right leg and hopping with my left, packing in that tense, quiet room. Luckily, Maya was still peacefully sleeping, as if she somehow knew I needed to focus. I've never been so focussed before or since. I was recording in my head every little bodily sensation, second by second, so that I could explain my symptoms to the doctor if I made it to the hospital.

At 11:30 a.m., my mom called again. "I've called you several times but no answer. Are you okay? Did you call Dan?" I calmly explained the rapid progression of symptoms, my decision to grab a taxi to NYU's ER with my dear friend Narumi and my plan to leave Maya with my other mommy-friend Nese, an Italian mother of a baby girl who lived in the same building. I still had not called Dan; I was using every second to prepare for my journey while I still had the strength.

"Okay," my mother said in her calm voice. "Go to the ER immediately. I'll book your father and me tickets to New York ASAP."

Narumi and Nese had dropped everything to rush to my apartment and they arrived before noon. By this time, I was having difficulty breathing. My numbness had spread to my left leg and nearly reached my diaphragm. I was having strong pain and squeezing pressure in my chest, making it even harder to breathe. I dropped all my weight on Narumi's shoulder and managed to hop out of the apartment on my left leg.

All this time, Maya kept sleeping as if it was any other Monday morning. There was no time to say goodbye or hold her in my arms one last time.

Nese gave me a gentle smile. "Don't worry about Maya."

The doorman of my building grabbed a taxi right away and helped lever me into the cab safely. I desperately tried to talk to Narumi about how to care for Maya. "Don't speak," she said, gently holding my shoulder and arm. "Save your breath and energy."

My mind was with Maya. I figured that by this time she was likely waking up and searching for me. *Hang in there, Maya.* The cab was moving slowly through midtown traffic on Forty-Second Street. Would going uptown have been quicker? My breathing was so laboured I thought I might die in the cab.

At NYU, Narumi ran out and came back quickly with a manual wheelchair she found. I could no longer stand on my feet, so Narumi picked me up and lowered me into the chair. As soon as we entered the ER, I was stunned by the sight of a huge waiting area filled wall to wall with patients, many standing or squatting as there were no empty seats. The ER had become the only medical facility in the US where patients had a right to care with or without insurance, so many of New York's uninsured used the ER as a walk-in clinic.

Narumi pushed my wheelchair toward the triage desk first but then quickly stopped and turned. She made a sudden a beeline through the "Do Not Enter" doors to the ER, screaming, "She is dying!" The crowd in the waiting area quickly and kindly parted like the Red Sea. The miracle lifted my spirits.

I bypassed triage and was immediately given a stretcher. ER doctors and nurses were swarming around me as I tried to describe the progression of my symptoms as accurately as possible. Through a gap in the curtains, I saw a woman in a white coat passing by. The next second, we were locked in each other's gaze.

"Keiko! What are you doing here?" It was Jane, my former neighbour from our apartment building on the Upper East Side, whom I had not seen for several years. I knew she was a social worker, but what was she doing in the ER?

"I'm working here as an ER social worker!"

Another coincidental miracle! Out of the corner of my eye, I saw Narumi multitasking: filling out the patient registration form while holding my overnight bag and winter coat, then phoning Dan and my parents. She was a busy mother of two boys around Maya's age, and I knew she needed to go home to them. I was so thankful to have a friend like her.

I urgently wanted to get diagnosed. My mysterious symptoms were advancing faster than I could have imagined. I was in the hands of a strikingly handsome ER resident-in-charge. He was doing his neurology residency and studying the mechanisms of paralysis under Dr. Doug Kerr at Johns Hopkins, the leading authority on transverse myelitis (TM), a group of rare disorders with a frequency of one to eight cases per million per year characterized by acute inflammation of the spinal cord and resultant neural injury. Although TM has an incidence of 0.0001 percent, the resident had a hunch and ordered the diagnostic tests, including a computerized tomography (CT) scan, blood tests and an MRI, and administered pre-emptive steroids. The inflammation was advancing quickly to my C5 vertebrae, which caused me a great deal of pain, numbness, weakness, loss of bowel and bladder control and breathing problems. I was grateful to be under the resident's care, but I was worried about the possible diagnosis. Spinal cord inflammation and a damaged nervous system was very bad news.

By the end of that day, I was transferred to a step-down unit (SDU), an intermediate level of care between the intensive care units (ICUs) and the general medical-surgical wards. Later, I learned that it would have cost me $10,000 USD per night if I didn't have health insurance. I had no idea then that I would be in the SDU for twenty-three days, followed by fifty-one days in a rehabilitation centre. My mind was on my baby. On that first evening, Dan told me over the phone that Maya had finally stopped crying and fell asleep without eating much. She must have felt that her mom had suddenly abandoned her. Instead of tears, I was expressing milk from my breasts onto my bed using my still-working left hand. It was extraordinarily painful inside and out.

In the SDU

The SDU had a nursing station and four patient beds partitioned by thin curtains hanging from the ceiling, as in a regular ward. During the day, the curtains were always open and I could see the sky and some buildings through the window from a distance. My bed was only a metre away from the nursing station, which had an open counter without any glass screen, so I could hear and see everything. The station was open 24-7 and two or three staff were always there. I could make eye contact and talk with the doctors and nurses. I wondered if it would be possible to sleep in this zero-privacy replete with lights and hospital beeps. I had never been hospitalized. I had never even stayed in a youth hostel. The other three beds in the ward had new patients regularly. For the entire month I was there, most of them stayed only one night, enroute to a general ward or ICU. I was, I felt, part of a survival experiment.

The resident diagnosed me with idiopathic TM the morning after

I arrived at the ER. TM is an inflammation of the spinal cord, typically characterized by paralysis—in my case, from the chest down. In a soft but desperate voice, I asked if he could bring me copies of all the published articles on TM; I urgently wanted to know what I was up against and whether there was any hope for a potential cure. He brought me about thirty peer-reviewed articles. I couldn't sleep because the severe pain and high-dose intravenous steroids kept me awake, and I read them all in a day.

Reading those articles was not a pleasant crystal ball. It was more like a misfortune teller: there were no cures on the horizon for TM. I kept searching, feverishly, for any sliver of hope, but there was nothing. Since the incidence of TM was so rare, there had never been any clinical trials. The information on prognosis was likewise slim due to the small sample size. Most published case studies I read were followed up for only six months, though a handful were extended for a few years. One paper documented an increased rate of depression among patients in the second year. *Oh, great*, I thought. *I have to watch out for that too.* I had enough to handle as it was.

Losing mobility was not something I had ever anticipated. Who does? The odds of contracting TM were around one in a million each year, but suddenly I was that one, unable to walk for life. At the time, coming to terms with this felt like a form of death to me. Over 90 percent of my engagement with the world was ambulatory, not only in how I functioned as a wife and mother, but also in my feelings of enjoyment, beauty and freedom. I couldn't even roll over on the hospital bed on my own now. I also felt like an outcast, exiled to a joyless, unknown world pierced by a deep anxiety for the future. Could I care for my baby and continue with the job I had worked so hard to get? How would Maya grow up with a wheelchair-bound mom? How could I show Maya my ballet moves? I had dreamed of taking ballet class with Maya one day, as my mom and I used to do. Would I survive? Would life be worth living? My life seemed to be over that day, December 11, 2006.

On his regular patient rounds, Dr. Weinberg, head of the neurology department, would cheerfully enter the SDU room and chat to each patient. I always prepared medical questions for him, but I also made myself presentable by applying moisturizer and some light makeup (mostly pink blush and pink lipstick). Makeup seemed so trivial but made a difference on how I felt about myself. Despite my perils, I remained calm and collected. He told me that he had never seen a patient with TM in his entire medical career and asked if he could present me in his case seminar and allow his residents to examine me. I declined; I could not bear the thought of being Patient A in a large room with all those eyes on me. I later regretted missing the opportunity to make that small contribution to the advancement of medical science.

Nonetheless, I had many specialists visit me every day because they were trying to differentiate TM from neuromyelitis optica, a rare inflammation of the central nervous system that results in blindness. My blood test samples were regularly sent to the Mayo Clinic for analysis.

One night, the ophthalmologist-in-charge visited me and sat beside my bed. Gently holding my hand, he cried and said, "We don't know much about this illness. Please help us." I saw an honest, caring human being in a white coat. His simple confession was surprisingly transformative. I imagined that I was holding hands with many people in the darkness, feeling brave. I was not alone in this fight.

On the fourth day in the hospital, Maya finally came to visit me, along with my parents-in-law, Eddy and Pnina, who had flown in from Vancouver. Over the phone, Dan had been giving me updates about how Maya was doing. I knew she was dispirited. I was so anxious to see her. The image of her rushing to me and crying "Mommy!" as soon as she saw me kept me strong. I could not wait to hold her. But when she arrived, she stood at a distance and kept her face down. She wouldn't even make eye contact with me when I called her name. She looked like a lost child. I was heartbroken. I was on a stretcher at a twenty-five-degree angle due to low blood pressure, covered in a white sheet and attached to many tubes and an oxygen mask. Did she recognize me? My heart filled with determination. *I must regain her trust.*

Dr. Weinberg and his team knew that maintaining my contact with Maya was of the highest priority. They rescheduled my medical and diagnostic appointments and personal care needs around a daily mommy-daughter lunch hour in the waiting area outside the SDU, which began on the fifth day. Shortly after, I began interviewing several potential nannies at my bedside and eventually chose Dechen, a young Tibetan woman. I gave her a detailed care plan written with my working left hand. Around the tenth day, Maya finally felt comfortable to rest on my tummy. And I held her tight as she fell asleep. I was in tears the whole time.

When she woke up, she cried and clung to me. "Mama." I cried for the short visit and for the victory.

The SDU visiting policy was amazingly generous. Visiting hours ran 24-7, so I could see my family and friends any time of the day. Although I spent Christmas in the SDU, I have no recollection of celebrating. My parents arrived in New York on December 28, prepared to stay as long as needed. They rented a furnished room at the NYU hospital's accommodation facility provided for patients' family members that was close to the hospital. They came directly to my bedside from John F. Kennedy International Airport (JFK), arriving late at night.

As soon as my mother walked into the room, I recognized her beaming smile and caring voice. "Keiko-chan"—an instinctual source of comfort and security.

I felt the flow of tears. "Okaa-san!" I cried out. Mom! It was hard to believe I was still alive and could hug her. She brought so many *omiyage*, little gifts, including a message board bearing heartfelt notes from my extended family, including my beloved ninety-two-year-old grandmother Tamiko. My tears were back. My mom removed my leg compression machine and started massaging my legs and back. Her hands never stopped. Like Maya, I fell asleep in the primordial care of my mother.

Many friends came to visit me. Sonja, a Serbian friend in her mid-twenties, came almost every night for a few hours. We talked, laughed and cried. Narumi often brought my favourite food, *unagi donburi* and rice balls filled with grilled salmon. Noriko, the mother of a daughter Maya's age, bought me comfortable clothing in preparation for rehab. Others—Takayo, Shirley, Rei, Jin, Akiko, Nese—came as often as possible. My colleague Linda, a cancer researcher in Arizona, reached out to prominent doctors all over the US to get second opinions when I had to decide between the many chemotherapy options.

One day, a neighbour in my building, whom I knew by sight but not by name, visited with a box of chocolates. "I heard about your situation from the doorman. Hi. I'm Ariel." We became close friends.

And I made new friends in the hospital too: doctors, nurses, technicians, nurse assistants, clearing staff. I was not sleeping much, so my nights were long. I would often chat throughout the night with the staff pooled around the nursing station, only an arm's length away from my bed, and we often laughed at our own funny and embarrassing stories, sharing the realization that we were not perfect.

Not all nights were social. I noticed at one point that a night-shift nurse in the SDU had a cold and was continually coughing through her mask. Sure enough, a few nights later, I began having a runny nose. At that time, I wasn't strong enough to cough: my chest and abdominal muscles were so weak I could hardly take a deep breath. Well past midnight, while lying on my back, my running nose filled my windpipe with phlegm. I immediately tried to cough, but nothing happened. I tried again and again. Trying hard to cough and breathe at the same time, I found myself choking. Panicked, I pressed the call button. The night-shift nurse eventually arrived. She quickly grabbed the suction machine perched above me and inserted a long, transparent tube up my nose and down my trachea. Then, she started manually moving it back and forth.

"It clears faster this way."

The sucking inside my airway was a dreadful sensation. I was still choking as I watched bloody liquid passing through the tube. I felt like a carp on a cutting board flopping up and down. *Is this it—just like that?*

As if a default switch had been activated, I found myself fighting to survive in every possible way. Eventually, the congestion was removed, but I was too exhausted to stay awake. I don't know how much time passed, but eventually I saw the dawn reflected on the glass building next door through the hospital window—a sliver of warm red against black. The sight felt miraculous. I was still alive and breathing, exhausted but strangely reassured. I was reminded of my favourite passage from *The Pillow Book*, written by Sei Shōnagon around 1000 AD in Japan: "In spring it is the dawn. As gradually the hills come to light, their outline is faintly dyed with red, and wisps of purplish cloud trail over them." We have so much in reserve.

My days at the SDU started and ended with heavy-duty medical treatment. I was given a week-long course of high-dose intravenous steroids, followed by a week of plasma exchange to cleanse my blood of inflammation. This procedure is similar to kidney dialysis: a tube is inserted "blindly" (without any imaging guidance) into a large vein in the neck. Through this tube, blood is removed, drained of its plasma and returned, suspended in a kind donor's fresh plasma.

As my graduation from the SDU approached, Dr. Weinberg proposed a final chemotherapeutic treatment option to get rid of any remaining inflammation that might take my life. Since there were no clinical trials of these chemotherapeutic medications, it was impossible—even for the specialists—to safely choose one, so I was the one who had to throw the dice. I consulted specialists from all over North America. I eventually decided to follow the advice of Dr. Traboulsee from the University of British Columbia's neurology department. I spoke with him over the phone from my bed. His exceptionally respectful and empathetic manner made me feel understood, heard and cared for and greatly helped me navigate this vital, difficult choice. He was the doctor who had seen the most TM patients—seven, I vaguely recall. So, I opted for mitoxantrone, and the good doctors at NYU administered it intravenously, three times total, twenty days apart, starting January 10, 2007.

REHABILITATION

January 2–February 21

It was my last day at the SDU, and I was graduating to the rehabilitation centre. With the kind help of a nurse, I was packing my few belongings... books, journals, a DVD player Sonja had bought me the first day, and my cosmetics! I found it amusing and perplexing that they were still one of my priorities in life, even during life and death moments. They seemed to bring out my life force.

I looked around this familiar room that had held me for twenty-two days, remembering how hard I had wished at the beginning that it was all a bad dream from which I could wake up. I had come so far, but I knew I still had a long way to go. I was still severely debilitated, unable to move or sit independently. When and how would I return to my family? The nurse gave me a big smile and a warm "Good luck." I thanked everyone, grateful for the life they had preserved.

My private room at NYU's Rusk Rehabilitation Center was at the end of a long corridor. In contrast to the SDU, I felt far from everything. Privacy did not mean much anymore. Looking at the call button hanging over my new bed, I wondered whether a nurse would come right away if I pushed it.

Then, Dr. Ahn entered and introduced himself. As a senior faculty member in the department of rehabilitation medicine at NYU School of Medicine (renamed the NYU Grossman School of Medicine in 2019), he was in charge of my rehab plan. He wore a suit and tie under his smooth white coat. At the SDU, most staff wore scrubs. On regular rounds, he was accompanied by a large group of doctors in rehab, pain management and other specialties, so I had a hard time remembering who was who. He told me I would need to be evaluated before they could plan my treatment.

The first thing I underwent was the American Spinal Injury Association evaluation, which grades the severity of a patient's injury. An energetic physical therapist and occupational therapist assigned to my case meticulously probed me from head to toe with a needle and a feather, which I could not feel. I knew it was essential for planning my rehab, but it was frustrating and discouraging to me; I felt as if I were failing a test over and over with no prospect of improvement.

Another difference from the SDU was that at the Rusk Center, I had to *work* at my many activities throughout the day. This included standing on a machine for a prolonged period of time, floor exercises for balance, turning in my bed as an exercise in mobility, weightlifting for my arms, occupational therapy for my fingers, practising getting in and out of my wheelchair using a transfer board, using my wheelchair (recommended during free hours) and learning to use an intermittent self-catheter. I still had side effects from chemotherapy, and a recurrent infection required prolonged use of antibiotics. I was exhausted all the time and rapidly losing weight: I dropped from one hundred pounds (forty-five kilograms) to eighty-five pounds (thirty-nine kilograms).

I often joked with my friends and said, "I survived my post-doc at Columbia, so I can survive all this." At least I didn't have to be judged by the gold standard of an Ivy League research university.

On particularly difficult days I wanted to play hooky, but my mom and Maya, who visited me every day, were my cheerleaders. Mom bought me colourful new clothes and dressed me up every morning, and Maya helped to push my wheelchair to the rehab room and stayed with me throughout my sessions. She was given the nickname Ms. ABC by other patients as she was always singing the alphabet song: "*a, b, c, d, e....*" I often heard patients asking, "Where is Ms. ABC today?" If it had not been for Maya, I would have skipped a lot of my rehab. I could not bear to act irresponsibly in front of her. No matter how hard I worked, though, I felt like I kept receiving F grades.

"I know you can do more, but you think you can't," Dr. Ahn said to me. "Or maybe you're afraid of trying." I knew he was right. I was afraid of trying hard because I was protecting myself from a deep fear: that I would never be able to walk again, no matter what I did.

It was mid-winter in Manhattan. Despite the severe weather, my father enjoyed walking in the city. He found a pizza shop nearby and often came back with a still-hot pizza for our dinner, excited and proud of how he communicated with the shop owner in English, accompanied by gestures. He must have seemed quite the character.

My parents noted my lack of appetite for the bland hospital food and they did their best. One time, in the middle of the night, they pushed a food cart on wheels into my room. I saw three large, covered bowls.

"I brought *keika* ramen," my mom said. "I made it in our little kitchen. It's still hot."

"WOW! My favourite!"

It was a sudden revelation to smell *keika* ramen again, a delicacy from my hometown. They had brought food from Japan in their suitcase! I imagined my parents carefully pushing the food cart with three ramen bowls perched on top across the snow-covered street as fast as they could.

"It's still hot," she repeated. And so, the three of us ate steaming ramen in the middle of the night, a Kumamoto family again. The taste was unforgettable. There were many beautiful family moments that month at the Rusk Center. My parents maintained their gentle smiles no matter what, which was the most precious and instructive gift.

The warm flow of friends continued. Emiko, my best friend from high school, now a medical doctor, flew in from Japan. She frequently appeared at turning points in my life. She stayed all night, massaging my back. She answered my parents' medical questions in Japanese. Dr. Ilya Kister, a busy neurology doctor, often stopped by to check on me. Sumika Ouchida, a Japanese nurse practitioner whom I knew from my graduate school days at NYU, came to reassure my parents that I would bounce back. I hoped she was right.

Spending three months in an American hospital was a challenge. A case worker told my husband that severely paralyzed patients, even those with health insurance, often become destitute within six months from the enormous medical and health-care bills, and that 70 percent of their spouses ended up leaving the marriage. This was a dark fear. In addition, a discharge plan was slowly emerging, even though I was not physically ready, so I started interviewing prospective post-discharge caregivers. I could not even turn on my own in bed; I would need 24-7 home care. I ended up hiring six people on rotating eight-hour shifts at a monthly cost of $7,000 USD out of pocket.

There was one last lesson I had to learn before being discharged. The Rusk Center had a life-sized model of a taxicab. Could I get from my wheelchair into the cab? A physical therapist demonstrated how to use the transfer board, a portable piece of equipment that helps you move from one surface to another, like a bridge. As I approached the model, I saw a huge gap between myself and the passenger seat. The board was barely touching the two supporting edges of the passenger seat and my wheelchair. I stared at the gap and could not hold back my tears. I was defeated by this tiny gap that would have been a non-issue for any ambulatory person. Since childhood, I had never cried like this in public.

"I can't," I cried. Then, Dr. Ahn's words crossed my mind. It was not just fear of falling; *maybe you're afraid of trying*.

My mom gently approached me. "It's okay. You'll be able to do it one day."

February 21, 2007, was the last of my seventy-four days in the hospital. I had received my last round of chemotherapy the previous day. My parents and Dan were there to help me home. I could hardly contain my excitement. I was feeling immensely grateful to the doctors, nurses and hospital staff who I felt had become part of me. I even wanted to thank the koi, goldfish, parrots, finches, canaries and doves in the Enid A. Haupt Glass Garden, a tropical greenhouse on the ground floor of the Rusk Center where Maya, my parents and I had spent so much time. While we waited for the taxi that was to take me home, I visited my tropical oasis one last time to say goodbye.

Dan assisted me safely into the taxi. I was crossing Forty-Second Street again, this time from east to west. The premature spring sunshine was so bright and caressed my face through the taxi window. I answered: "I am coming back alive!" The noise of New York traffic serenaded me. While waiting for the light at Fifth Avenue, I saw crowds of people enjoying the day. I had been there once.... A small surge of grief momentarily compressed my chest, but the overpowering anticipation of seeing Maya's lively face brought me back.

BEFORE THE CRISIS

1994 Onwards

I sometimes wonder whether the *mitsuba*—my good luck charm—had something to do with originally drawing me to New York, the City of Dreams. Whatever the cause, I was lucky enough to relocate to the city with my husband shortly after our wedding. I met Dan through a mutual friend in Tokyo. A Harvard-educated Jewish Canadian, he had just completed his PhD in political science at Princeton University. We were married in Vancouver in 1994 and quickly moved to Manhattan to start a whirlwind life together. We were the same age and, curiously, had the same blood type: AB. Some Japanese believe an old wives' tale that a person's blood type was an indicator of one's personality. In fact, we had vastly different personalities, but he was honest, kind, well-read, considerate, hard-working and kept his promises. And, what I liked most of all, he was a great communicator. He spoke French and Japanese fluently, which was a relief for my parents. I had never met anyone like him, and my world quickly expanded beyond what I could have ever imagined. He told me that he wanted to create financial freedom for our future child so that one day he or she could pursue becoming an artist should it be desired. As a child, he grew up worrying about money. I was hardly aware of my own needs at the time, let alone those of my future kid.

Newly arrived in New York with my caring partner, I was swimming in a wide cultural river. The endless shock of the city was like opening a new birthday present every day: the Met, the Museum of Modern Art, Guggenheim, the Whitney, Lincoln Center, Neue Galerie, off-Broadway theatres and Central Park. Nothing could be taken for granted. I was excited every time I stepped outside.

I was also fermenting my dream of becoming a researcher. I was working towards a PhD in community health sciences at NYU. From 2000 to 2002, I was a research assistant for the World Cities Project

(WCP), a joint research project between NYU and the International Longevity Center (ILC) led by NYU Professor Victor Rodwin. From the ILC office building, only a five-minute walk from our apartment, I collected and interpreted data about aging populations in Tokyo. I loved working there.

I was fortunate enough to be invited to travel with Dr. Rodwin to London in November 2001, and to Paris the following year for the WCP international conference, where experts from New York, Paris, London and Tokyo were to share new research regarding how to meet the needs of an aging population.

But the fall of 2001 was not an easy time to fly. On 9/11, I watched black smoke rise from our Upper East Side apartment. My knees were buckling. Dan left half an hour earlier than usual that day, as he had an important meeting at 8:30 a.m. To get to his office in the World Financial Center (WFC), he had to go through the passageways under the World Trade Center. The first plane hit the North Tower at exactly 8:46 a.m. I couldn't get a hold of him until the end of the day as all communication lines were down, but I spent that time furiously trying to believe that he made it to the WFC by 8:30 a.m., as he was always punctual. By the end of the day, I learned that he was safe. I was delirious with joy when he returned home undamaged. But if he had not had the early morning meeting, he would have been in those passageways beneath the World Trade Center at 8:46. There are no words to describe what he meant to me.

My flight to London for the WCP conference was scheduled for November 13. On the twelfth, an airbus flying the same route to London crashed on Rockaway Peninsula in Queens. There were two hundred and sixty people on board and no one survived. The flight attendants outnumbered the passengers on my flight to London. My colleague Michael and I sat next to each other in the mostly empty plane. As soon as we took off, we stared out of the porthole to look for the wreckage site. Within a minute, we saw the large patch of burned ground below us. All the aspirations wrapped in that airplane had evaporated in a fiery instant. I focussed on my mission, full of anticipation for the London conference.

London was a whirlwind. I walked along the Thames after midnight; ate ramen with Dr. Rodwin and Michael; saw the play *Stones in His Pockets* (though I missed the British humour); and stayed in Goodenough College in the heart of Bloomsbury. Dr. Rodwin even had a surprise encounter with the Queen, who visited Goodenough the day we arrived. Michael and I missed her by a few hours. Meeting collaborators from all over the world who came to celebrate our shared mission was a most rewarding experience. The work presented at the WCP conference in London, and the conference a year later in Paris, would culminate in a book publication in 2006, and I was to author a chapter entitled "Long-term Care in Tokyo: Home or Institutional Care?"

I graduated NYU in 2002 and shortly afterwards landed a three-year post-doctoral fellowship in cancer epidemiology at Columbia University. The contributions I made were tangible, and so was the validation I felt. My workdays were filled with research: I carried a heavy bag full of papers to read on the subway on the way to Columbia and, once there, analyzed data and wrote papers, ate lunch at my desk and drank countless cups of coffee, attended and presented at conferences and seminars, worked at home after dinner... and again and again, day after day. I thought I was living to the fullest, though sometimes I felt I was swimming as hard as I could in a sea of unbridled competition. I was a little *medaka* swimming among bigger fish in an ocean too large to comprehend.

Then, in the spring of 2005, I gave birth to a precious baby girl. I was thirty-seven and had almost given up having a child while working in academia, but my lucky *mitsuba*, it seemed, was still with me. We named our daughter Maya (舞弥) to symbolize growth and strength. The combination of Chinese characters means "to spread around" and "to prevail."

Nearly four months after I gave birth to Maya, I started a blog in Japanese called *Curious Maya*. It was a way for me to invite my mother, father, sister and friends in Japan into my new world. I was not just writing about motherhood and the joyful and terrifying surprises of being a first-time mom; I also wanted Maya to have a meaningful early history when she was older. And maybe I was also writing for my own future self, who might need to rediscover something that had been lost.

THE DEBUT

The big playground debut arrived when Maya was four months old. Every Tuesday morning in the summer, there was an open playdate organized by some local mothers living in Hell's Kitchen. We had moved there six months previously from the Upper East Side, where Dan and I had lived for ten years. My new neighbourhood had a different ambiance: there was a strong queer community, a mix of ethnicities and many different struggles and dreams, a little bit like *West Side Story*. There were four playgrounds of different sizes and with different amenities close to our new apartment. For all mothers with small children, playgrounds are like air or water—you can't live without them.

On our first Tuesday morning playdate that summer, I nervously opened the gate and gingerly pushed Maya's stroller into the playground. Large trees cast shade over us and it was suddenly much cooler. I saw a dozen mothers and a few fathers—all wearing a relaxed, lived-in look, not a common sight in New York—who seemed to know each other. Dressed as an uptown girl, I was an alien presence. I slowly walked toward a swing with Maya snuggled against my chest in her BabyBjörn carrier.

"Hi! I'm Pia!" A blonde mother gave me an inviting smile. Soon I was surrounded by friendly mothers, all from elsewhere: Russia, Sweden, Bulgaria, France, the Midwest and Japan. Pia, a Swedish mother of two, gave me her phone number and invited me to a playdate with her daughters. She told me about her hobbies—Korean martial arts, karate and Flamenco dance—as she exuded warm, radiant smiles. By the time Maya and I were on our way back home, my nervousness had vanished. So would my uptown look, eventually. For Maya, it was the beginning of social life.

Learning to Be Both

The University of Arizona Cancer Center in Tucson invited me to present a talk on correlations between social support systems and cancer screening behaviour. The invitation was important for my career, and I knew I had to try my best to make it. My colleague Dr. Linda Larkey was a research assistant professor there at the time, and she helped me scheme a journey to Arizona with a breast-feeding five-month-old who refused to drink bottled breast milk. It felt impossible.

Linda and I had met two years earlier at the American Association for Cancer Research (AACR) conference in Phoenix. We hit it off right away; we shared similar research interests in health behavioural change in cancer prevention. At the conference, I received the AACR Scholar-in-Training Award for my research, which was later published in *Health Psychology*. I also received job offers from a few universities, which I politely declined. I had to look for an academic position for after my post-doc somewhere in Manhattan. It was not an easy prospect. The job-hunting stress was constant, and as I prepared for my talk in Tucson, I felt the anxiety intensifying: I was nearing the end of my three-year fellowship with nothing yet confirmed for afterwards.

Under normal circumstances I would have travelled alone, but Maya changed all that. Luckily my husband volunteered to travel with me, so we made it a four-day family trip. It was mid-September and the temperature in Tucson was 39°C. I had no idea whether it was wise to bring a baby.

We booked a flight to Phoenix; from there, Linda was to pick us up and drive the two hours to Tucson. On the flight, we coincidentally sat next to Dr. Ruth Westheimer, an American sex therapist whom I had seen on TV. Her infectious smile was unmistakable. We chatted and laughed non-stop throughout the five-hour flight. She was enchanted by Maya and played with her as if she were her granddaughter. Jotting down on a piece of paper her address and phone number, she asked me to send her my research paper—and Maya's photo. I promised to do so. Maya's presence made the world much gentler and pleasantly surprising.

The next morning, the alarm rang at 4:30 a.m. I was already up, getting everything ready for 6:30 a.m., Linda's arrival time. I glanced at Maya's things I had neatly packed in her diaper bag: sunscreen, toys, clothes, and her car seat. I gently woke her, changed her, breast-fed her and dressed her, then made coffee. On the hotel coffee package, I stared at an image of cactus in a red desert. We were in the Wild West. I encountered those cacti on the road to Tucson. Looking through the car window, I was mesmerized by how large they were, spread over the vast desert. Japan felt very small.

The morning traffic jams made me nervous. By contrast, Maya was happily asleep in her car seat. It was nearly 9 a.m., when my talk was scheduled to start, when we arrived at the Cancer Center. I made it, but just barely.

"Good luck!" my husband called to me as I climbed out of the car in a hurry. I turned and made eye contact with him. He looked the epitome of the supportive husband and father. I gave a quick nod in thanks; I was already putting on my professional look. All my focus was now on my presentation.

The presentation went as planned, as did Maya, who happily interacted with new people, new floors, new furniture, who knows what else. Thanks to Dan, I did not have to worry about her during the conference. I was absorbed in my work. Juggling work and motherhood, I continually felt I was dropping one ball while throwing another in the air. Some kind person usually caught the balls that dropped.

When the plane landed at JFK, it was dark and drizzling. Maya had not slept throughout the flight and immediately started crying. Once we returned home, I got her relaxed and settled into her crib. It was a long, uncomfortable journey for such a little one, and I was proud of her regardless of the restless tears.

"Sweetheart," Dan called, "come up to the terrace!"

Once Maya was sleeping, I met him on the terrace. Our jasmine tree was in full bloom. Beautiful white flowers dotted the tree where it had been bare four days ago. I smelled the sweet, fruity scent of jasmine mixed with the earthy aroma of fresh rain. The tree looked happy, as though it were welcoming us.

"*Tadaima!*" I responded. I'm home.

THE WAVES OF OUR EMOTIONS

"Keiko, do you have a time for coffee this afternoon?"

I was leaving a seminar at Columbia University when a colleague approached me with the invitation. An MD/PhD, he worked at the Irving Medical Center and the School of Public Health. He was highly successful and looked my age.

"Yes," I replied, startled. Since I began my post-doc, I didn't know anyone who had time for a coffee break. We met later, several blocks away in a café that was not a normal Columbia hangout. I arrived on time and saw him already seated. He ordered cakes and coffee for us.

For a while we exchanged office gossip, then he said, rather abruptly, "Keiko, I'll tell you my secret." He paused for a moment. "Do you know what my fear is?"

"What do you mean?" I asked.

He leaned over the table. In a low voice, he said, "I fear I'll be discovered to be mediocre."

"*What?*" I was floored. He not only had an impressive list of publications but was also a principal investigator on several sought-after grants and a practising physician with office hours, which would secure his academic employment even if his research faltered.

"Honestly? Then how should beginners like me feel?"

I don't know what motivated his revelation, but I was grateful he shared it with me. Academic competition was fierce and draining; I understood where he was coming from, even though I was a smaller fish. I felt a strong sense of belonging.

Around this time was the one-year anniversary of the death of Rob, my husband's closest friend, like family. He was in his early fifties when he died of lung cancer. Rob's wife, Lei, organized a get-together in their beautiful Upper West Side townhouse. Over two hundred family members and close friends from around the world attended. We all spoke our memorial tributes in turn. The sounds of weeping came in waves, interspersed with laughter.

I remember Rob's presence, great sense of humour, warmth and keen powers of observation. He resembled Jack Nicholson. I was initially intimidated by his intense, perceptive eyes, but soon he was making me laugh. He would tell me how happy he was about my marriage. He noticed things I was wearing. "I like your scarf, Keiko. You look like Audrey Hepburn in *Japanese Holiday*!" he joked, grinning broadly. During my morning commute in the crosstown bus, I often spotted him riding a bicycle flying along like an elegant bird.

"It's okay to cry, Keiko." I remember Rob saying this to me as he was dying, watching me weep beside his hospital bed. "I'm so happy to hear you're expecting," he continued, breathing heavily, extending his arm toward my belly. I was four months pregnant at the time.

As I massaged his ice-cold feet, I couldn't stop myself from sobbing.

"My heart feels very warm," he said gently. The aggressive form of lung cancer was starving his body of oxygen, leading to gangrene. His feet were already black, as was half of his nose. I couldn't imagine what it was like to witness one's own body decaying.

During our last visit, I sat and looked tearfully into his eyes, holding his arm with my hands. His fingertips were black too.

He smiled. "Thank you. Please take good care of your baby." His face was so beautiful.

In a few days, he was gone. I will never forget his grace—while he was alive and as he departed.

My Favourite Improv Moment

Pushing Maya around in her stroller with Dan in Hell's Kitchen on a warm, sunny winter afternoon, I felt peaceful and complete. I wanted nothing more. Passing by a basketball court adjacent to a newly built Hell's Kitchen playground, I saw a group of ten boys, aged five to fifteen, playing basketball. They were speaking a Middle Eastern language, and their lively voices were bouncing from the court to the walls of the surrounding buildings, as if they were composing music.

"Can I join you?" I impulsively shouted, taking off my winter coat and handing it to my husband. An older boy looked me as if everything was normal, then he threw me the ball. I was in the game at that exact moment. I was running and following the ball mindlessly, watching the bouncing boys in my peripheral vision.

"Hey, here! Here!" I shouted, just like them. We called each other with some hand gestures and occasionally made eye contact to communicate. The sounds of our voices, the bouncing ball and our sneakers on the pavement reverberated together. We ran up and down the court countless times. Our shadows were overlapping and parting like a shadow dance. Catching my breath, I realized that I had become carried away: I had played for thirty minutes, leaving my husband and my baby in the stroller on the bench. I loved playing with a ball when I was younger, but I had never done something like this before. "Thank you!" I shouted to the boys. They waved their hands.

"Why did you do that?" my husband asked as I approached him. He handed me my coat.

"I don't know!" I answered, flushed.

"I really like your spirit!" he added.

It just *happened.* I couldn't remember what I was thinking when I tossed Dan my coat; my body was moving before I could think. I'll never forget that moment. No names or conversations were exchanged, but the boys' shining, innocent eyes and the goodness in their hearts toward a stranger who wanted to pass the ball around with them for a little while became the defining impression of my neighbourhood.

In Spring It Is the Dawn

March 2006

I woke up early to find a strawberry-tinted sky through the window. Our white bedroom wall turned soft, orange-pink. Momentarily, I thought I had slept until dusk, but my alarm said it was 5:30 a.m. I jumped out of my bed and went downstairs to get my camera. By the time I got back to my bedroom, the room was becoming purplish pink. The sky was changing by the second, with drifting clouds growing whiter and lighter. Mesmerized, I kept taking photos.

"In spring it is the dawn that is most beautiful. As the light creeps over the hills, their outlines are dyed a faint red and wisps of purplish cloud trail over them," I quietly recited to myself in Japanese. My favourite line from Sei Shōnagon's *The Pillow Book*. It comes back to me every spring.

This time, I rephrased it: "The light creeps over the *city skylines*, their outlines dyed a faint red, and wisps of purplish cloud trail over them." A sudden wave of nostalgia swept over me and I felt like crying. *How often had I seen this beautiful spring dawn?*

Maya was born around this time a year earlier. She was only five pounds (2.27 kilograms) when she was born. She fit perfectly in my two hands. Over the past year, I woke up as often as I needed, every few hours. Maya cried whenever she was hungry and cried a lot for her other needs too. Every night was long. It was physically exhausting but emotionally exhilarating. I was often still awake before dawn, and I could watch the light creep across the sky like a dancer entering the stage. No matter how exhausted I was, the grace and subtlety of the spring dawn brought me to life. In Japanese culture, the word *yūgen* describes an emotional awareness of the natural world too deep and powerful to translate. Thanks to Maya, I never missed experiencing the *yūgen* of the spring dawn. The only words that spoke to my condition were those of Shōnagon.

Maya was becoming cuter and more active and energetic by the day. She was like a little bouncing ball. I made a commitment to stay in shape so I could keep up with her. As I tried to balance motherhood with my career, I was noticing myself being pulled toward spending joyous time with Maya. I had recently submitted my fourteenth publication with a great sense of achievement, but Maya was a huge disincentive for staying in academia. What was next?

Dan had a business trip to Singapore planned, and we decided to go as a family and stop in Japan so we could introduce Maya to my grandmother Tamiko. The non-stop flight from JFK to Singapore was nineteen-hours long, but we travelled first class and relaxed comfortably on a seat that turned into a 180-degree flat bed. It was a flying carpet. Maya was snuggled under my armpit and was able to nap or breastfeed at any time, just like at home.

On the first night in Kumamoto, my parents and many relatives gathered in the living room of my grandparents' house and we shared stories and laughed over delicious meals and drinks. It was as it had always been.

At one point in the evening, I realized Grandma wasn't in the living room. I saw the sliding door that connected the living space to an adjoining room half-open, so I approached it, entered the dark room and found my grandmother sitting alone in the middle of the room.

"Ba-chan, what are you doing here? Come join us and eat. This room is cold," I said.

She smiled and replied, "Maya is crawling in and out."

A moment later, Maya came charging through the opening of the sliding door, crawling full tilt on the tatami mats with sparkling eyes and a gleaming smile. She was headed straight toward her great-grandmother like an arrow through the dark.

Tears came to my eyes as I understood what I was witnessing. This was an example of Grandma's compassion and awareness of other people's point of view—even a baby's, even when inconvenient. She was devoting herself to Maya's happiness in this moment and Maya seemed completely at home; she had quickly found a kindred spirit.

This was the same compassion my grandmother had shown as she raised me. I remember how I used to play wildly with my friends in the garden, clothes covered with dirt. Grandma would always sit on the sun-filled veranda facing the garden, watching me with her gentle smile for as long as she could, as if she were available to me all day. When I was in kindergarten, I wrote my name all over her dresser with an oil-based marker pen. It was not a prank; it simply came from admiration of my Ba-chan. I used to play alone in front of her dresser for hours, pretending to groom myself as a lady. Grandma was never upset with me and kept my graffiti.

That memory of Maya charging into the room towards her great-grandmother has always stuck with me. There was simple grace and elegance in the silence between my grandmother and Maya—a deep love that I can only call "soul language." The half-open sliding door symbolized, for me, the window to the nature of being that invited Maya to freely explore. I was happy she could communicate beyond words with my grandmother, even though it was brief and possibly the last time. I would remember it all my life.

The Biggest Crisis

May–June 2006

Maya had been lifting her right arm and hand toward the sky constantly for several days. Something was strange. Instead of her usual high-spirited smiles, she seemed lethargic. No fever. She had never been sick except for a low fever two months prior. What was happening? In an abundance of caution, I took her to the Ryan Chelsea-Clinton Community Health Center a block from our apartment. By the time the nurse Jess, who knew Maya from birth, examined her, Maya was more lethargic and a bit feverish. She was still able to breastfeed. Jess immediately arranged an ambulance to take Maya and me to a nearby hospital. Maya was closing her eyes, as if she was falling asleep. Soon she became unconscious.

Dan and I stayed overnight in the mid-sized hospital as Maya awaited diagnosis. I held her hands by her bedside all night. After blood and cerebrospinal fluid test the next day, we were transferred to another hospital, one that had a pediatric critical care facility. Maya was immediately put in the negative-pressure room. Soon, it was past midnight.

The diagnosis was pneumococcal meningitis. Maya had been vaccinated against pneumococcal meningitis when she was six months old, but the vaccine she received did not protect against the strain that infected her.

A pediatric specialist approached us and said, in a serious voice, "Be prepared. One in four kids don't make it."

I was hardly able to breathe. How do you prepare for that—for a 25 percent chance of losing your daughter? I was too traumatized to cry.

I was permitted to stay in the negative-pressure room with her. She was still in a coma. I slept on a cot the hospital provided next to her bed for nearly two weeks. Dan regularly delivered me dinner, lunch and fresh clothing.

Being with Maya in the negative-pressure room at night was a dark time. I cried alone. Seeing her adorable sleeping face covered by monitors and tubes, I thought, *If you don't make it, neither will I.* I really meant it. I imagined walking the street like a ghost where I had once pushed a stroller full of joy and hope, and I couldn't bear the idea of outliving her. I would not and could not live one day without her. For the first time in my life, I couldn't predict whether I would have another to-morrow. I held her in my arms as long and as often as I could. I watched her intently, especially at night.

One afternoon, the breathing and heart-rate monitors suddenly started beeping. They were turning red. She was suffering a severe seizure. Swarmed by doctors and nurses, Maya was turning dark purple. There was white foam coming from her mouth. The first injection to stop the seizure failed. The air was tense. The doctors scrambled. Death seemed imminent. The oxygen saturation level in her blood was 70 percent—far too low. I was panicking. *She will have brain damage if she survives....*

The nurse standing next to me suddenly said, "Do you want me to help your husband?"

"What?"

She pointed to him. I swiftly looked up and saw him outside the negative-pressure room pacing back and forth.

"Yes," I replied, then turned back to Maya's face and squeezed her right hand, trying to use that soul language to communicate to her. *Please, Maya.* It was the most intense fear I have ever experienced.

The second injection to stop the seizure succeeded. Maya's face gradually became less purple until it was pale but calm. Her coma lasted about a week, but it felt like a month. I never left her bedside.

When her eyes finally fluttered open, she would not respond to my call. She looked foggy. Her CT and MRI scans showed some effusions in her subdural space—a collection of fluid trapped in the narrow space between the surface of the brain and its outer lining, a common com-plication of pneumococcal meningitis. The buildup of fluid can cause pressure on the brain and possibly brain damage. The doctor-in-charge seemed relaxed about it and explained that the effusions might regress or be absorbed spontaneously and would not require surgical interven-tion. I was not convinced, however, and started searching for a second opinion. I reached out to a surgeon at Columbia University who special-ized in this area. He immediately responded and recommended drain-ing the fluid to lessen the pressure in her cranium. He miraculously of-fered to come to Maya's hospital to do the procedure, given how critical her condition was. We arranged the surgery with the full force of our negotiating skills.

The morning after surgery, Maya woke up and responded to my call as if she could hear everything. She voiced "mama" clearly. It was a miracle. It was as if the sun had come out after a month of nighttime.

Her fever was still coming and going as an after-effect of the inflam-mation, even though the infection was gone. Her weight had dropped from 17 pounds (7.7 kilograms, the fifth percentile) to 15.5 pounds (7.1 kilo-grams, the first percentile) by the time of discharge. She had permanent-ly lost her hearing in one ear too. However, in one day, she regained her incandescent smile and deep curiosity. We were extremely happy to have her alive. After three and half weeks in the hospital, Maya was discharged.

In the meantime, a new problem was ravaging our home. Dan had been making sure that our penthouse apartment was safe for Maya to return to, as the roof had been leaking for about six months. He hired a mold specialist to test the quality of the indoor air and, shockingly, they found a high concentration of toxic mold (stachybotrys), which made it impossible for us to return to our beautiful home.

For the following month, we lived in a hotel room that had a sep-arate living room for Maya to play in. We were under doctor's orders to keep Maya indoors for at least a month after discharge. The hotel suite was quite an upgrade from the hospital's negative-pressure room, but well worth it. I continued caring for Maya, taking a leave of absence from work, while my husband took care of everything else, including dealing with our mold-infested apartment and hunting for temporary housing. Our friends often came over to cheer us up, bringing food, toys and light.

GETTING BACK TO NORMAL

The Summer of 2006
"What's your name?"
    "Maya."
    "What a pretty name!"
    "Thank you."

Eighteen-month-old Maya enjoyed conversing with strangers on the street. Every time she saw a stranger, she started saying, "Mama, mama," while pointing her index finger toward me to let them know I was her mother. I smiled bashfully at the passerby.

Life was finally getting back to normal. We were still displaced from our toxic mold–contaminated apartment. We lost most of our belongings—our furniture, clothes, shoes, all our books and paper files, jewellery, hats, family albums and treasures. The only things we salvaged were our laptops and some artworks that were covered by glass and could be wiped and decontaminated. We decided to temporarily move to a furnished condo nearby to build a new nest as we fixed our old one. Our new apartment was small but adequate, and the building came with its own outdoor playground and a rooftop terrace atop the forty-one storeys with a 360-degree view of Manhattan. Maya made a few great friends, Bella and Melissa, who lived in the same building. The whole building became her new nest.

One of Maya's favourite words was "NO!"—though I had heard that this was a necessary and healthy step in growing up. She said it a lot more than I would like. Maya already had vocabulary of 108 Japanese words (yes, I counted). Even though she could not hear in her right ear, her speaking and comprehension was more than superb. A specialist told me that her brain was cross-wired because she was left-handed: in lefties, the parts of the right and left sides of the brain that process language work in better tandem. She didn't seem to want to give up my breast milk yet. Her weight was back up, close to normal. Every day, I fell in love with her again and again.

The Florida–NYU Connections

October 2006

A professor in the department of epidemiology at Florida International University asked me at the end of my last post-doc year if I would be interested in taking an assistant professor position in his department. I politely declined. He subsequently reached out to me again to ask if I would reconsider, as the position was still open. I again politely declined. Most academics move wherever the jobs are. Deep down, I knew I didn't have a clear, long-term goal nor a burning drive to stay in academia. I was treading water in an academic sea, next to the financial lifeboat of my husband's career. Despite my disciplined life, I felt I was missing something, especially after becoming a mother; I just didn't know what. After chatting about my feelings with my husband, he suggested a short family vacation to Florida. We booked five nights at The Breakers in Palm Beach to pamper ourselves and enjoy family time.

In Palm Beach County, we visited the Morikami Museum and Japanese Gardens. I was transported by its scale, expansive collection and authenticity, and surprised to find it on the edge of America. We spent a whole day walking the eight-mile-long path that wound through the two-hundred-acre garden. The garden originated from the vision of Japanese native Jo Sakai: after graduating from NYU, he returned to his hometown Miyazu and then brought a group of pioneering Japanese farmers back to Palm Beach to create a farming colony, intending to revolutionize agriculture in the early 1900s.

"Because of that aspiring young man, now we can enjoy this! And he was an NYU alumnus too!" I exclaimed. I was moved by what he managed to create in pursuit of his ideals, far from home, at the turn of the twentieth century. I felt a great sense of romance begin to overlap my own ongoing migration. Feeling refreshed and rejuvenated, we returned home.

Upon our return to New York, I received an email from the director of continuing studies at NYU. I was invited to give a two-hour lecture in November and to possibly co-create a summer course in health-care management. Health-care management had become an increasingly important and intellectually exciting field, although I had no practical experience in it. I said yes to both; it would be good to venture out of my comfort zone. A century-old connection between Japan, Florida and NYU had inspired me.

My Last Photograph Standing

Through a mutual friend's referral, I was asked to pose for the New York–based photographer Adam Friedberg for his series *NY no Nihonjin*. It had been a while since I had been photographed by a professional: shortly after I moved to New York, I was scouted on the street for modelling. My husband encouraged me to try it for fun, so in between my studies, I went to auditions and did some work as a movie extra. One cold day in February, I was photographed in Central Park wearing a red

Chinese dress. A small boy came up to me and asked for my signature. How embarrassed I was!

On November 5, 2006, Adam came to my apartment for the shoot. Adam was very tall, laconic and gentle. *NY no Nihonjin* was not for commercials; the series was meant to document real people going about their lives, and I was instructed to be as natural as possible, to be at home in my normal living environment. He placed a chair near the window where a lot of Maya's toys were randomly tucked against the wall. After he gave me his initial instruction, he didn't say a word throughout the shoot. He just kept shooting behind the black curtain attached to the camera. I tried to be natural, which was harder than I thought. I didn't smile and instead began to think deeply about my life. I realized that 2006 had been the most challenging and the happiest year in my life yet.

Two weeks later, the large prints of my portrait were delivered to me. "Oh, dear, I look so sad and serious!" I felt disappointed in myself. Indeed, the person in the portrait looked tense and alone.

I called my sister in Japan. "Is this how I look naturally?"

She kindly said, "It reminds me of a young leaf in springtime."

"Really?" I was perplexed. "How did you get that impression?" How Japanese she was.

The year was coming to a close. It was the most dramatic year I had ever faced, for better and worse. I had no clue what was awaiting me. Lying in bed alongside Maya and Dan, I noticed that we formed the shape of a river expressed in Kanji, Japanese characters: 川. I looked at Dan's face as he was falling asleep. He looked exhausted. He was our fighter and provider, and he had been dealing with the huge challenge of our water-damaged apartment.

"Dan, I couldn't be happier than I am now," I whispered. Everything I wanted was right here, right now. I closed my eyes to catch some sleep before Maya woke me, unpredictably, to be nursed.

My grandmother's words came to my mind. In grade six, she had showed me a blue button from my kindergarten uniform that she had carefully saved. She attached it to her wallet with a string.

"Taking care of you when you were small was the happiest memory of my life," she told me in Japanese, while gently rubbing the small button that I used to wear every day. Lying in bed with my family, I understood what the button meant to her.

A New Manhattan

BARNARD

March 2007–August 2009

Shortly after I returned home from the Rusk Center, a letter arrived from the Barnard Toddler Center, an integral part of Barnard College's psychology department. I was surprised. Prior to my illness, I had heard great things about the Toddler Center from a colleague at Columbia. And, as soon as Maya was old enough and the application window opened, I picked up an application package. Glancing at the lengthy form, I was impressed by the details it requested: how Maya was conceived, her developmental milestones, parents' educational background, life experiences, etc. The centre was an academic institution with a dual purpose: to provide initial social experiences for toddlers and to conduct research on early childhood development. It required detailed information on the parents as part of the research. "It feels like writing a thesis!" I half-jokingly said to Dan.

That was when I was suddenly thrust into NYU's hospital system for nearly three months. Accordingly, I had not completed the application form nor submitted it in time, but while I was fighting for my life in the hospital, Dan had gotten a call from the Toddler Center. They asked him why I hadn't sent the application back and he explained what happened to me, and he was told to fill out the contact information without completing the rest and to send the form back as soon as possible.

I opened the letter: Maya was accepted! I was in shock, as the Toddler Center was competitive and selective. I was grateful that they had amended the application process for us. I imagined my two-year-old daughter and I flying back and forth together from our new nest at the Toddler Center that had just taken us under its wings.

This thought was a pleasant distraction from acclimating to my new life at home, which was a series of new challenges and adaptations. My privacy and independence were distant memories. We privately hired 24-7 caregivers, as I still could not even turn on my own in bed and was physically weak. Due to exhaustion and constant physical pain, I was hardly able to sit for three hours at a time on a manual wheelchair that the hospital had given me. I was learning how to use intermittent self-catheters to empty my bladder, but it required some caregiver assistance at the beginning, as my right hand was still numbed, painful and immobile. I managed to learn to write with my left hand and became quite good at it.

I hardly went outside for the first few months post-discharge, so our friends came to visit me. I was often amused by the wide variety of their expressions when they saw me in my wheelchair for the first time. Most of my Japanese friends did not stare at my wheelchair or my compression socks and did not ask direct questions. While they must have felt discomfort, they treated me as if nothing had changed. My Israeli friends, though, asked right away, "What happened to your legs? Can you move or feel?" I was surprised to find that I appreciated both styles—the Israeli practical empathy (not rudeness) and the Japanese code of respect and honour (not indifference).

I had my own contradictions as well. My cheerful smiles, partly driven by a sense of duty to family and friends, displayed my skill at Japanese, bento box–style compartmentalization. Inside, I felt shame at having become a burden.

Some three months after my hospital discharge, my life was transformed by an electric wheelchair donated by the Alan T. Brown Foundation, thanks to their director, Fran Brown. I could finally go outside on my own and reclaim my independence. Learning how to use the chair—and reclaiming that independence—was a slow process. I felt some embarrassment initially, but that soon evaporated. Nearly everyone passing by gave me warm smiles.

By the time September arrived, I was just sufficiently recuperated to sit in a wheelchair for four or five hours at a stretch. I was getting somewhat better at using the catheter myself while seated, although it always required focus and attention. Using Access-A-Ride, New York's public wheelchair van service, I commuted twice a week to the Toddler Center with Maya and my caregiver. When we arrived in the morning, I loved looking up at the elegant, cream-coloured stone building entrance where 119th Street and Claremont Avenue meet, which bore the name BARNARD in capital letters.

In the classroom, we were greeted by a whole new world. This included all the energy and wisdom of a collective of great women (and sometimes men): the head teacher, Leslie; the founder, Pat Shimm; the director, Dr. Tovah Klein; and all the committed mothers, including a few high-profile names like the Seinfelds. I spent a lot of time together with this diverse group of people in the classroom, the two-way mirror observation room, the tiny room where the parents' weekly educational sessions were held (led by Pat), the playground or at each other's homes for playdates. I soon learned that the Toddler Center wasn't just for toddlers; I belonged to a stimulating, intentional and resourceful learning community.

I also learned a great deal about how toddlers see the world, process emotion, negotiate with peers and use play to make sense of their world. The teachers seriously addressed the issue of separation anxiety for both toddlers and mothers, so all mothers or caregivers were required to sit against the wall of the room and observe the class for the first six weeks or so. It was a once-in-a-lifetime chance to see my daughter engage with a group of willful two-year-old children in a room full of toys—and without any adult intervention. Among the parenting lessons I learned, the one that stood out the most was the importance of free play, especially outdoors, advocated and researched by Dr. Klein. The teachers prepared homemade edible playdough, for example, adding just the right amount of hot pepper so that toddlers could safely learn on their own that playdough was not for eating, rather than halting their learning with censorship or an upset stomach. I watched with amazement how Maya kept her enthusiastic focus on interacting with all sorts of toys in the room, without a trace of boredom.

This observation period demanded discipline from us parents! At the first few classes, Maya did not want to leave my lap, as she was intimidated or uneasy in the new environment. Leslie immediately noticed and asked me to let her go. There were also many moments that made us hold our breath—such as when Maya picked her nose and discarded her boogers onto the shoulder of a boy who happened to be standing next to her. All mothers were watching the scene from the mirror room. I turned my head to silently apologize to the mother of the boy, and Maya and the boy continued to play as if nothing had happened.

Whenever I was at the Toddler Center, I always felt something mighty, expansive and hopeful, like hearing the strong fetal heartbeat from a mother's womb. At first, I wondered whether it came from the centre's commitment to evidence-based science, or perhaps it had something to do with the unleashed potential of each toddler whose future was happily developing. But soon I began to wonder whether it was because my own creative energy was awakening as I watched my toddler explore and create so freely. I, too, was learning how to engage with a new world. My future was also developing.

It's sad to leave a place you love. When Maya's graduation day finally came, I cried in front of the head teacher, Leslie, during our one-on-one teacher-parent meeting.

"I sincerely respect you, your strengths and confidence, which are reflected in Maya," Leslie said. "Maya is 'spicy,' meaning she can stand up for herself and express her will freely, which is very important for growing up."

The spice in the playdough was now serving as a good metaphor for a secret ingredient to supporting the whole self. This spice looks different to each of us, and I was beginning to understand that my spice was my commitment to developing a playful nature essential to artistic creation. The Toddler Center taught me how to identify, with empathy, the power of my imperfect body. Closely watching the kids throughout an entire year, I learned to see each one as a unique and precious being, and how the right environment and nurturing enhanced human development. I hold Dr. Klein's advice on free play near and dear to my heart.

Preschool

I met Lesley Nan Haberman for the first time during our preschool admission interview at the Montessori preschool Family School West (FSW) in Midtown Manhattan. I was seeking to arrange Maya's post-Barnard preschool and had sent applications to four or five schools. Dan, Maya and I went to the parent-child interview at FSW together and I was nervous, as if I were applying to university. I was definitely a first-time parent.

At the beginning of the interview, Lesley noticed my wheelchair and asked what had happened to me. It was rather abrupt, but not obtrusive. I sensed a compassion in her that is hard to put into words. Once

I answered, she shared with me her own health condition and associated pain as if I were her close friend.

The following day, I received an email from Lesley: "You glided through the room like a gazelle.... You are a courageous young woman and I know that one day you will be able to do all the things you wish to do.... The love that you spread, just by being yourself, will help you to overcome all obstacles now in your path." I was incredibly moved. Her email was not only unexpected and touching, but also confirmed my daughter's admission and asked me to serve as a class parent.

Without having to think, I said yes. Shortly after my discharge from the NYU hospital, I felt as if I were a returning soldier who lost his limbs (functionally, at least) in the war, but the miracle of being alive made me aware of how precious life was. I was gradually becoming more confident getting around the city in my electric wheelchair and, after Barnard, I felt like I was ready for the next step, just as Maya was. I felt encouraged and validated in Lesley's warm presence. I was still quite limited physically and learning to adapt, but she saw through my vulnerability and gently gave me back the confidence I needed. Who wouldn't be drawn to people who treat us this way? I was deeply touched.

At FSW, students were engaged in a wide-ranging and stimulating curriculum, including foreign languages, songs, violin lessons and cooking. Lesley gave me permission to exercise my free spirit as a class parent and independent woman—that is how I interpreted and made coherent sense of her warm gestures, words and expressions. One activity I helped organize was flower arrangement. How illuminating it is to expose pre-kindergarten children to flower arrangement! Although the two formed an unlikely combination in my initially limited mind, watching both together—the wondrous eyes of the children and colourful petals of the flowers—drove me to creative action. I knew a little bit of *ikebana*, the Japanese art of flower arranging, but one day, the idea of recycling unsold, expired but still-beautiful flowers entered my mind. Within the radius of a few blocks from FSW, there were four stores selling fresh flowers. I went to each one and pitched my idea and one of them said yes. My weekly pick-up of a huge bucket full of flowers and its delivery to FSW began that day and continued for the rest of the school year.

I soon realized that I had become a bit of a scene on the street in the middle of Manhattan: a huge bucket full of flowers resting on my lap as I pushed through foot traffic on a motorized wheelchair. It was not only heavy and hard to balance on my lap, but also tall, blocking my frontal view, so I had to tilt my head ninety degrees to drive. I was fearless, reckless, fast and joyful. I must have looked comical, but I was frequently showered with warm cheers and encouragement on the street. I often stopped and chatted with strangers and was touched by their kindness. Passersby were metaphorically and figuratively stopping to smell the roses, and so did I. I was aware of my surging sense of freedom, of being alive, every day.

And of course, the surprised and curious faces of the children every time I entered the classroom with my colourful cargo were priceless. FSW teachers were always grateful for and creative with my "catch of the day." Once in December, I brought a bunch of bare tree branches (all that was available), wondering if they were usable. The moment they saw the branches, which looked as if I had collected them from a wild, winter forest, the teachers broke into big smiles. "We can use this for learning about seasons!"

The ladies at the flower store became familiar faces. At the end of the semester, we gave them a certificate of appreciation that the students made and some potpourri and small bouquets of dried flowers that they had created from the donated flowers, which made them tear up.

One day, a young woman I knew before my diagnosis told me, out of curiosity and good intentions, that she would be frightened to travel outside on her own if she were wheelchair-bound and that I was very brave. I smiled and replied, "I used to think that way too."

At that moment, I realized how much I had changed my sense of self. I no longer felt that able-bodied people were invested with a superior sense of self. I felt I had witnessed my entire neighbourhood become one living organism. Local café staff on my commute up Ninth Avenue started exchanging morning smiles and afternoon waves with me every time I zipped past them—even on the days I wasn't delivering flowers. People were giving me a big thumbs-up, saluting my park ranger hat and leather boots, which I wore every day, even during the summer.

"Love your boots!" they sometimes shouted.

"Thanks!"

In Hell's Kitchen, I was stopped by strangers eight or nine times a day on average. They would ask me if I needed any help even when I was simply waiting for a traffic light to change. Everyone became my peer.

All my interactions within my community brought me a sense of safety, trust and inclusion.

The compassion of Lesley and other friends and strangers, their simple acts of kindness, was key to building a new community. But they also changed the way I saw myself in a wheelchair and how I understood my new identity. They helped provide a sense of freedom from my previously held stigma about disability. I was affirmed, nourished and liberated, and the community forming around me also changed. We were all transformed. My neighbourhood was somehow becoming an extension of myself.

I think of Lesley as a kind of universal role model. She was carefully observant, stood strong among friends and colleagues and brought me in to be nurtured; slowly, I began "standing" with them too. Lesley reminded me of one of the most beautiful Japanese expressions: *yorisou* (寄り添う), to "snuggle up" with someone or stay close. But it carried more than a physical meaning, implying acting together in solidarity, connecting with people's lives and hearts, coexisting harmoniously. It's about symbiosis, understanding and empathy, and our community grew because of this. If I ever encountered conflict again, I would remember to flex my *yorisou* muscles.

An Artistic Process

I often took Maya to Le Carrousel in Bryant Park, only fifteen minutes away from our apartment by wheelchair. The same old Filipino man was always there working as the customer service representative. Every time he saw me and Maya at the ticket counter, he would signal with his kind eyes and hands to waive the four-dollar fee and let Maya ride for as long as she wanted. Every time I tried to pay the fee, he just shook his head with a silent, gentle smile and I would bow my head in gratitude. Maya knew nothing of his gift, but she was always happy, going round and round without care.

Dan and I often ate out, but most New York restaurant entrances had some sort of steps, making it hard for a wheelchair user to get inside. Ten times out of ten, I would be spotted by customers seated along the sidewalk who would get up and carry me inside immediately, without being asked.

In the summer of 2008, I started bringing Maya to the Met's free art program for kids, twice a week. Dennis, a volunteer, was exceptionally attentive. He always made sure that Maya and I had a pleasant experience despite the crowded room. After the program, Dennis would spend his lunch hour playing with Maya and other kids outside the museum steps near the water fountain. Maya and her three-year-old friends would chase Dennis with jubilant exclamations, then climb up on his strong shoulders like acrobats. Dennis and the kids were kindred spirits.

He often brought me a toy or stuffed animal from the museum shop. "This is for Maya," he would say, handing it over discreetly.

I often thought that the New Yorkers I encountered because of my wheelchair were compensating for my injured legs and torso in a kind of informal balance. I understood then the weightless sense of giving and receiving. I did not know at the time, but this was the artist's process at its best—its most heartful and generative.

Lost in Numbers

The two-year mark was approaching since the onset of my TM-induced paralysis. I happened on some data from a specialist at Johns Hopkins on the life expectancy of patients with TM: they lived seventeen years, *on average*, after the onset. This was induced from a small sample size so it did not mean much, but it shocked me to the core. I quickly did the math. *Does that mean I'll die when Maya turns nineteen?*

This was an emotional time. I had expected to live well into my nineties given my Japanese genes. Time is the most precious thing in life. Had I lost thirty, maybe forty years? The rare autoimmune inflammation had damaged my spinal cord and my body and it was now invading my rational mind, robbing me of hope.

How ironic it was for me, who spoke the language of probabilities and health outcomes as a profession, to contract this extremely rare condition. I no longer thought I could see—let alone plan for—the future. For the most part, I hid my sense of despair and failure well, even from myself. But when I read published scientific papers discussing longevity or disease prevention, an overwhelming sense of loss would wash over me. For a little while, I developed an allergic reaction to statistics.

A Big Move

At the end of the summer of 2008, Lehman Brothers, one of the biggest investment banks in the world, filed for bankruptcy. Wall Street called it the Lehman Shock and the rest of the world called it the 2008 Financial Crash. My husband was then a managing director at Sagent Advisors, an investment bank specializing in mergers and acquisitions. Even though these types of firms were not particularly vulnerable to the sub-prime mortgage crisis, it felt like the end of the banking industry. We feared Dan's career was insecure, and with it our family's savings—and my medical insurance.

Dan had worked diligently for the previous fifteen years and we were careful with money. We often talked about future retirement plans: six months in New York, three months in Vancouver, where he was from, and three months in Paris. He was forty and had been considering early retirement, but my condition was a complication. There was another factor: Maya would be ready for kindergarten the following year. For a private school, tuition would exceed $20,000.

At that time, I was spending much of my waking hours processing health-care bills from hospitals, private doctors and specialists. Despite my insurance coverage, I was often required to pay out of pocket if care providers were in a different managed care system than mine—another US health-care trap. I started thinking about Canada's public health-care system and the free tuition offered by Vancouver's decent public schools, particularly the French immersion and International Baccalaureate programs.

"Let's move to Vancouver!" I suddenly said to my husband one day. It was a promising prospect. I only wished I could bring our whole extended New York family with us.

The following year, January 2009, was the harshest winter I had ever experienced. The Hudson River froze solid. All the ships, big and small, were frozen in place. With the unobstructed view from my thirtieth-floor Midtown apartment of the ice-clogged Hudson River, all the way to the George Washington Bridge, I imagined I was about to set out on an Arctic expedition to the edge of the unknown world: the West Coast, Vancouver, Canada. It felt like the edge of the world. I recalled American jokes about how provincial Canada was. Was I making a premature decision to leave a place I love and my many friends? The sight of icebound ships disturbed me. Nonetheless, Dan agreed with my proposal to move to Vancouver, and we started looking to buy a house there.

One February afternoon, the phone rang. The gentle and familiar voice on the phone was that of Dr. Traboulsee, the neurologist who recommended which type of chemotherapy to choose at the end of my stay at the NYU hospital. He was attending a conference in New York for two days.

"I would like to visit you if you're free for a few hours this afternoon. By the way, call me Tony."

What a coincidence! He was the first person I wanted to meet in person as soon as we arrived in Vancouver. Despite his busy schedule, he had called us many times to ask if there was anything I needed. Before my injury, I was a total stranger to him. The kindness of people like him was changing the way I thought about health. Before we met that afternoon, I baked an apple cake for us to share. I surprised myself. I felt more secure knowing he lived in Vancouver. I imagined being warmly welcomed there.

FIREWORKS

The move to Vancouver was finalized, and our final day in New York was to be the last day of August 2009. The countdown was on. Throughout June, July and August, I spent every day as if it were the last, frantically organizing farewell lunches, dinners and outings with every friend. Three months was not enough.

As the pressure grew, I created a website that provided an online version of *yosegaki*, a collective message board that normally exists as a single, square sheet of paper. Japanese people write *yosegaki* messages on special occasions. Many friends participated. One friend wrote: "Keiko, your departure makes me feel that I lost something precious, knowing that I won't run into you or your family on the street anymore. We know that you will bring the same kind of spirit to your new home city." It served as a gentle push: "Yes, you can do this."

The summer was incredibly full. The Fourth of July fireworks celebration was held in the Hudson River to mark the four-hundredth anniversary of its exploration by Henry Hudson, and I watched the celebration for the last time from our apartment with a few close friends. We had an amazing 180-degree view of the most spectacular fireworks

I had ever seen, right before my eyes, as if to celebrate our time and memories of New York.

Mesmerized by the vivid colours, many memories came and went. I had a flashback of my first ride in a yellow cab shortly after immigrating in 1994. I raised my right hand to catch a cab like a New Yorker but didn't know that I had to open the door because Japanese taxis have automatic doors. I stood for a moment, waiting, then the driver yelled at me, and at the time his voice had sounded just as powerful as the sound of the fireworks. He was a bit harsh, but it was a funny welcome to New York. It was a fond memory. Watching the fireworks outside my apartment window, I sat quietly in my wheelchair, tears running down my face. I already missed it all. "Thank you and goodbye," I murmured softly.

Five friends came over for dinner on our last night. We shared warm candlelight, animated conversations, yummy New York pizza, smiling faces, intimate voices and long hugs. Three of them stayed overnight on the floor to escort my family to Newark Liberty International

I long to capture the ephemeral beauty of the ever-changing sunset sky, a mesmerizing experience akin to immersing oneself in a captivating symphony. *A Tapestry of Vibrant Memories*, 2021

Airport for our 7 a.m. flight, and to then return to our apartment and tend to the piles of boxes that had to be shipped to Vancouver. What did I do to deserve this deep care and protection from our friends? Holding back tears, I tried to pretend that this was not our last pizza date. I was overwhelmed—too many feelings at once. I was going and coming, saying goodbye and hello.

Up to the very minute our plane took off, my time in New York was illuminated with the light of mutual love. I was preoccupied by one clear image: Dan, Maya and me sitting in a tiny boat perched on the shore of an unnamed beach. Then, singing and cheering us on, our friends push the boat out to sea. I palpably felt that sensation of sliding on the wet sand and then suddenly being lifted, losing my sense of balance on the surface of the water. I opened my eyes and wiped my tears. The plane was taking off. Seeing the Manhattan skyline from above, I whispered, "This is it."

IKIGAI

On August 31, 2009, we landed in Vancouver and my world changed. Though it was the end of August, Vancouver's summer felt like New York's fall. The air was crisp and cool. New York's hot, humid air was laden with many different smells, and I usually had to carry a handkerchief to wipe the sweat off my face and occasionally cover my nose. Here in Vancouver, I smelled... what was it? Trees?

We settled in a furnished condo near Granville Island while we renovated a house in West Southlands to make it wheelchair accessible. We stowed our luggage in the condo and I then immediately took Maya to the playground in front of our building. It was triangle-shaped and had no fences but was surrounded by many trees. In contrast to my fatigue, Maya was energized as soon as she saw the playground. The playground was empty. *It's practically private!* I thought.

Soon, I spotted a mother with a toddler. I approached and said hello. The mother was friendly but did not reveal much about herself. After some quick chit-chat, I wrote down my new phone number on my old business card and asked for her number, suggesting a playdate. For one reason or another, she did not give it to me. *What just happened?* In New York playgrounds, mothers were often exchanging numbers even before conversation, as socializing was so important to a toddler's healthy development.

I remembered the words of my dear New York friend Shiuga, a Japanese American married to Greg, a descendant of the Akimel O'otham, previously referred to as the Pima Nation. She was a professor at a local community college and a mother of three amazingly talented kids. She was working on a book called *Navigating the Playground*, and she had told me that a playground teaches us everything we need to know. I already felt nostalgic for the hustle-bustle playground and my friends in New York. Cool wind gently touched my cheeks. As I watched Maya playing alone, I whispered, *I will find your playmates soon.*

An Artists' Salon

As I was preparing the move to Vancouver, I began to worry that my wheelchair might create social barriers. In Manhattan, we had lived in a tall apartment building with an elevator that diminished physical barriers. I could visit my neighbours freely. Even though Vancouver has a reputation as the most-accessible city in North America, we were moving to a detached house in a neighbourhood populated by other detached houses, most of which were not wheelchair accessible, making it hard for me to visit my new neighbours. Could I get them to visit us? If I could solve this, Maya and I could be part of a living community again. In Japanese, the hard-to-translate word *ikigai* refers to an individual's sense of his or her life's purpose or chosen direction. My *ikigai* was evolving. I found myself giving priority to finding and forming human relationships.

The new city came with new routines. Every weekday, Maya and I would take a wheelchair-accessible bus to her preschool, and then I would sit and wait for her in a quiet café for two or three hours, reading books and newspapers. One day, in January 2010, I came across a short essay in *The Globe and Mail* called "I've Joined My Mother's Club" by Laurie O'Halloran.[1] The writer, a middle-aged daughter, was recalling childhood memories of her mother who had formed a little community by starting a book club. The daughter followed her mother's footsteps when she started her own book club as an adult, and it also grew into a small community, just as her mother's had. I was touched. I imagined my own grown-up daughter writing something similar someday. I promised myself I would give Maya a gift like this: the rich experience of a community, whose value I fully understood. I brought the newspaper clipping home with me as a token of my promise.

But what kind of little community could I start? I had always loved the concept of the salons in the French Enlightenment and those Gertrude Stein held in early twentieth-century Paris because of how they encouraged the crossing of boundaries: while they were predominantly attended by the upper class, the salons nonetheless presented opportunities for bridging social and intellectual barriers between the nobles and bourgeoisie. Hosting a salon at a private home, like those free-thinking women in Paris throughout the centuries, had a strong appeal to me. A salon it would be—once the renovations were complete and we moved into our new home.

A few months later, my husband and I were invited to speak at a private salon given by the former Vancouver mayor Sam Sullivan at the Opus Hotel in downtown Vancouver. What was a private salon? Was it similar to the French salons? All Sam told me was to prepare a thirteen-minute speech about my passion. Without hesitation, but not fully understanding, I said yes, entirely out of curiosity. I had been reasonably confident speaking in public if the subject had concerned my research, but this speech was about who I *was*. I was nervous. I had only two weeks to prepare.

Around the beautifully set dining table in an elegant room at the Opus Hotel, nine invited guests sat for a formal dinner. We had each prepared a talk. I felt like a fish out of water; the guests included the principal of a landscape architecture firm, the head of psychiatry at St. Paul's Hospital, the chief of external relations for the City of Vancouver, a media company president and philanthropist, the president of the Liberal Party of Canada and others. I was intimidated by the elitism and formality.

Sam was at the head of the table and I sat directly to his right. To my right sat Omer Arbel, an industrial designer who was selected to co-design Canada's 2010 Olympic medals.

Sam looked at me, smiling, and said, "Keiko, why don't you go first?"

My talk began with a question I had been wrestling with since moving to Canada: How can social connectedness improve public health given the rising problem of social isolation in Vancouver? At Columbia, I was interested in the links between supportive social connections and cancer prevention, especially the design of community-led support systems. Community engagement had become an important topic for my research.[2] At that time, however, the extremely high demands of the academy meant I didn't have the time to participate in community activities myself.

I spoke candidly at the salon. All eyes around the table were on me. "My own tragic event, which confined me permanently to a wheelchair, opened many doors for me to experience a community, a wider community that I hadn't known existed. I lived what I had been preaching during my academic life; I finally got to put the theory into action!"

After my speech, many people spoke about what they had heard and what connected them. I felt gratitude and appreciation to everyone at the table. I left feeling inspired.

France's Enlightenment and Modernist salons encouraged sharing and interpreting art. My salons were to be similar. In September 2010, one year after moving to Vancouver, I began hosting a cultural salon roughly twice a month in my newly wheelchair-accessible home. My goal was to gradually grow these salons into intergenerational celebrations of community creativity. I started by inviting our new friends and neighbours, then artists from all over the city. I named it the Artists-in-Residence Salon, or the AIR Salon for short.

Maya was five years old when the AIR Salon started. Although I strongly believed that children should be seen and heard, I was unsure of how Vancouverites would react to the addition of five-year-old children to an artist salon. Luckily, all the guests were warm, welcoming and engaged with those willful children. The youngest kids always began by sitting together in the first row to listen to the presentation; then they dispersed as they got bored.

At the beginning, I used to approach interesting-looking strangers on the street and ask them what they were passionate about, just as Sam had asked me. It worked 100 percent of the time. After hosting the first fifty salons or so, I no longer had to scramble to find presenters. Soon, salon regulars started giving me recommendations or volunteering themselves as presenters. "I want to support what you are doing," they would say. I didn't really understand *what* I was doing for the community at the beginning; I was following my intuition. But the salon community was busy organizing itself, sometimes without my active intervention and sometimes propelled by happy accidents.

The AIR Salon has neither rules nor fees; all I ask is for people to bring something for the potluck. After the doors open at six o'clock, guests flock in with dishes and drinks, often homemade. I love this moment. It feels like opening a box of chocolates. Our kitchen fills with delicious smells and warm laughter.

Around 7:30, I ask everyone to slowly make their way to the living room. Attendees finish up their chit-chat and food, then gather for the presentation of the day. I often witness the evening's presenter sharing and discussing her or his work even before presenting it.

In the living room, the presenter waits patiently. We sit in a circle of couches, sometimes in rows, depending on whether we're using the projector and screen. I dim the lights, the conversation ceases, I introduce the presenter and then she or he begins.

I am careful to keep the space safe, to make everyone feel welcome and to allow them to take creative risks and explore vulnerability. I reserve lots of time for Q&A and group dialogue. Sometimes, the presenter and audience members exchange roles: the presenter prompts the sharing of an audience member's art, for which the presenter then expresses appreciation. The audience does much of the creative work of interpretation—becoming, in a sense, co-creators. I often feel as though I am visiting a new playground. New ideas, motivation and perspectives always emerge.

For the last salon of 2010, I invited Omer Arbel to give the presentation. He claimed that he prefers the word *make* to *design*, which he finds cold. As he put it, "The act of making involves a really direct interface with the project, which results in very strange and unexpected things. We all eventually become the reason for the object to be meaningful." Long after the salon ended, I remained preoccupied with the process of *making*—the invisible, creative process resulting from juxtaposing people and objects. His remark resonated with me; I interpreted it as "art for life's sake," which I believed in, for art can illuminate the complexities of our shared experiences.

The Locket Necklace

In late December of 2010, Dan, Maya and I flew to New York for a week to take care of some unfinished business and see old friends for Christmas. Daily stresses were accumulating, and my relationship with Dan was unfortunately growing strained since we moved to Vancouver. The idea of going back to New York to see familiar faces, even if only briefly, was refreshing. We scheduled outings with as many friends as possible; every lunch, teatime and dinner during the week was reserved for friends.

One day I visited my old neighbourhood, Hell's Kitchen, to have lunch with a mommy-friend. As I was rolling down Tenth Avenue, approaching the area of my former apartment, I saw a young man running toward me and waving his hand. I looked behind me, as I thought he was waving to someone else.

"Hey, do you remember me?"

It took me a moment. "Oh, you were... our superintendent?"

"I'm really sorry for what happened to you," he said with a gentle and sympathetic tone of voice. He reached his hand into his pocket. "I found this on the floor in the hallway when they were moving all your stuff last year. I kept it just in case I might run into you."

I gasped in surprise at what I saw in his hand. It was my heart-shaped silver locket necklace, in which I had carefully placed a photo of my husband and me when we were much younger. I used to wear it as often as I could. I had forgotten all about it.

I was speechless. Did he carry this all year long, hoping to one day return it to me? I was so touched, not only by his humanity but also by the sudden serendipity. I thanked him earnestly.

I also felt pangs of sadness and anxiety. I had been happily married for sixteen years, but I wasn't sure how I could get Dan and me back to being the happy couple I saw smiling in the heart-shaped locket.

After returning to Vancouver, I put that locket in a jewellery box in the glass display case in my closet so that it would never get lost again. What would I have done without my family through all the turbulence of the past three years?

A WARM COINCIDENCE

One hot summer day in 2012, a typical school day, I was rolling up the slope of Dunbar Street in my motorized wheelchair. I was on my way to pick up Maya. The steep slope, about 800-metres long, was my everyday commute to her elementary school and the grocery store. Because of the steepness, I moved slowly.

I heard a car horn behind me, turned in my chair and saw a white SUV passing by. I didn't see the driver but thought it might be a friend, as my mommy-friends sometimes said hello that way. Once I reached the intersection at the end of the slope, I saw the same white SUV parked curbside. A middle-aged woman behind the wheel rolled down her window and waved at me, smiling open-heartedly.

"Hi!" she said. "I wanted to say hello. I always see you on Dunbar Street, going up and down, sometimes with your little daughter on your lap. I have painful arthritis in my hands, but every time I see you on the street, rain or shine, it lifts me up!"

"Oh, thank you! Do you live in the neighbourhood? Would you like to come over for tea sometime? I should get your number." I was touched by her kind heart and delighted to meet a new neighbour so spontaneously.

She gave me her card, and I recognized her name. "Oh, Gail Sparrow... are you the former Musqueam Chief? I've been wanting to meet you!" I had joined the board of directors at the Kerrisdale Community Centre in 2010 and learned how the Kerrisdale area is on the unceded land of the Musqueam People.

This serendipitous encounter started a close friendship. I invited Gail to present at the salon and she was happy to; she talked about her family story as well as her vision for the Kerrisdale Community Centre. Every time my parents visited from Japan, she would bring them to the Musqueam community, show them around and invite them to her and her sister Debra's home. Without needing much interpretation, they connected with hand gestures and laughed together over meals. My mother always brought Gail Japanese green tea from Kumamoto (it became Gail's favourite!) and performed Hawaiian dances for us in an authentic costume to recorded music.

When my mother passed away in 2019, Debra Sparrow showed up at my front door and gifted me a Musqueam blanket folded into a square.

"Gail just told me about your mother," she said, looking straight into my eyes. "You're our family. We're family."

I often think of Gail as a Vancouver incarnation of Lesley from Maya's preschool in Manhattan, as the ways we met were so similar: the wheelchair helped catalyze the happy, chance encounter of two women.

SALON 100

Unexpectedly, I was chosen as one of Vancouver's twelve Remarkable Women in March 2014 because of the AIR Salon. The Vancouver Park Board started this program in 2008 to honour women who had made significant contributions to the community. I could not believe my luck—all I did was the simple act of opening my home!

Nervously, I spoke in front of a large audience at the ceremony. "My hope for everyone and myself is to develop a lifelong passion for learning and creativity, serving others and bringing our inner beauty to the world." At the ceremony, I quietly pledged to live up to the standards of the award.

The hundredth salon was approaching around this time. One day, two of my friends, Deborah (a musician) and Isabelle, who had already presented, approached me, smiling broadly, as if they had a plan. A few years ago, the three of us had self-formed a still-active book club around Julia Cameron's book *The Artist's Way.*

"Keiko," they said, "we think it's your turn to present. Say yes!"

Oh, no! They are testing me!

No one had ever said no to my request to present, so how could I possibly say no to them? The salon slogan was "We're All Artists," although I never fully embraced this idea myself—at least not at the start. It was about time I started seeing myself as an emerging artist. I shyly said yes.

I thought deeply about what I should say. *Who am I now?* I thought. I had studied epidemiology at Columbia and I was still studying it in a sense, but this time I included myself as a study subject. I was becoming much more independent, developing my own set of methods and ideas for creating social support networks. And I was becoming more resilient, like an artist. But what was my medium? My medium was people, I realized, specifically people from the little community I had... had what? *Built* was not the right word. The community had always been there, ready to self-assemble. I felt more like a flower arranger or a midwife than an engineer. I prepared a sequence of slides and a speech about the recent events of my life and my feelings of gratitude toward the empathic people of New York and Vancouver who had supported me when I most needed it.

The day arrived. Over fifty people came to listen and celebrate our milestone. After my presentation, I asked guests to share their reflections and their own memorable experiences with the salon. Many people stood up one by one and spoke from their hearts. Some wrote and recited a poem, some sang an original song and some used humour. What people expressed in response revealed much about how the salons had transformed them.

My friend Aimee, a mother of two and one of Maya's elementary school teachers, said, "Everything you do is so positive, and really, when you retire, you've got this younger generation of kids, students, that will carry it on... especially Maya. ... I [will] see her carry it on into the next generation.... I've loved it. It has changed my life, so thank you."

We all shared her sentiments about future generations, as there were about seven kids sitting on the floor listening. I looked around the room and I felt I was, once again, surrounded by the kind of empathic, creative people I had known in New York, only this time we were in Vancouver. The evening felt liberating—it became one of the most memorable events of my life.

Vancouver was a friendly city in many other ways as well. All the buses, for example, were designed so that wheelchair passengers faced the rear of the bus and backed their chair against a padded backrest. Accordingly, when I was on the bus, the other passengers were all facing me, often with eye contact. By design, it naturally created interactions. One day, I was on a crowded bus with twelve-year-old Maya. When the bus suddenly braked, I spilled a cup of milk on my boots. I saw some hand movements and something white coming toward me from the back of the bus, floating on an ocean of hands. Finally, a person sitting in front of me passed the white thing to me. It was a fine cloth handkerchief. Who would carry such a thing these days? And how kind! I looked for the culprit and saw the big smile and waving hand of a teenaged boy in a private school uniform. How gentlemanly! I used his fine, white handkerchief to wipe the milk off my boots, feeling the gaze and cheers of the audience on the bus. I smiled back without my normal Japanese sense of shame, finally comfortable with who I was in this city.

After Salon 100, I asked a few salon presenters—including Maya, at the time in sixth grade—to reflect on their experience at the salon in short, reflective essays. Maya wrote a long, detailed essay, elegantly capturing the importance and benefits of community formation and expressing her gratitude for being included. What more could a mother ask for? I never anticipated this from my twelve-year-old. Every time I read it I am moved to tears. Unlike Laurie O'Halloran's mother, I did not have to wait for years to know that there was meaning growing in my struggling life. I was glad to have pushed forward. Maya's essay was germinating within me. I kept it as if it were a precious letter from the future.

A Japanese proverb states, "planted peach and chestnut seeds take three years [to bear fruit]; persimmons take eight" (桃栗三年柿八年). It means that it can take time to see the fruits of our actions. Nearly five years and one hundred salons later, and after meeting many hundreds of attendees, the seed I planted in 2010 had indeed borne fruit in many minds. But how did the AIR Salon stay so fresh over the years without passing into decay or decadence? The second law of thermodynamics can help answer my question. AIR was not a closed system; it drew energy from outside and created a state of steady flow, where people came and went freely and shared an ethic of openness. They took the liberty of bringing not only knowledge, skills, wisdom and creativity, but also their friends and social networks. Each salon had a different central theme and new people who brought new connections and education. Nothing ever stagnated.

Shortly after Salon 100, my marriage ended at the nineteen-year mark. I became newly single. This was involuntary, unexpected and devastating, as my marriage had been the most sacred sanctuary and refuge for me in my wheelchair life. I had not only lost my mobility, career and possessions, but I was also forced to change from "happily married" to "single, part-time mother." It felt as if I were splitting my daughter in half. I could not shake off my dream of going through life with Dan. Since the age of twenty-six, we had been comrades, sharing challenges like 9/11, our daughter's life-threatening illness and my paralysis. Even after the lengthy divorce, I still loved and admired him. But I now had to become the one I relied on completely. I had no choice.

Co-creation

The salons continued to thrive and develop, and I soon found myself creating a non-profit organization called the Vancouver Arts Colloquium Society (VACS). Our mission was to create opportunities for community members to experience contemporary art as audiences *and* as creators. By reaching across social boundaries and encouraging people to share personal and creative struggles, VACS aimed to not only reveal the illusory nature of some societal constructs based on differences, but also release the forces of social change. I had no professional training in the arts or in management, and my education—public health and epidemiology—had uncertain value in this realm, but I jumped anyway.

My friends Daniel Conrad and Oliver Hockenhull, accomplished filmmakers, played a significant role in forming and growing VACS, as well as influencing my sense of identity. They were my reliable wingmen. Daniel helped draft the mission statement, our Declaration of Independence. Always calmly spoken, he was observant and succinct and had a penchant for "finding beauty in natural patterns," as he put it. He supported everyone in need, creatively and empathically. Oliver also got involved in VACS from the beginning; he passionately led the VACS team with his critical consciousness and mystifying sense of beauty, and he was always charming and the best dressed in the room. Many of his touching personal messages made me feel beautiful and capable. Behind every great woman are great men, I can say. My bond with them grew stronger over time.

I also joined the board of the Kerrisdale Community Centre Society to learn about my neighbourhood. I soon noticed that there were no community programs where we could learn about the Indigenous culture of our neighbours, my new friend Gail Sparrow's Nation, the Musqueam. Nor were there any programs through which Musqueam and non-Musqueam could build genuine relationships. The other board members mostly seemed content with the status quo. I was not. I approached Gail and she agreed with me that the board should reach out to Musqueam members, consult with them and include them in its programming decisions. Changing institutional inertia was not easy. It occurred to me that art-based programming would be particularly useful for promoting inclusion.

In 2015, I received federal funding for my newborn non-profit, VACS. I used the funding to develop a novel participatory art project called *Creative Weaving* with Debra, Gail's sister, a Musqueam weaver. In later years, we received additional funding from the City of Vancouver, allowing us to expand the project as a sustainable, intercultural weaving workshop series that we called Weaving Our Way (WOW), which soon found a home at the Dunbar Community Centre.

Debra encouraged participants to be both unique and cooperative. "I am all about staying unique," she would always say. We used the method of co-creation not just as a technique but as an embodiment of community. Co-creation was compatible with Debra's self-identification as a messenger: "I didn't want any teachers except for my ancestors. I call on them. We're storytellers. Artists carry history. They are visionaries responsible for reflecting culture, and my hands are merely receiving my ancestors' messages."

Under Debra's direction, many weavers, myself included, conducted our own ancestral research, bringing fabric from our own cultures to a workshop, comparing them and finding common designs and shapes. I brought a picture of my family crest, called Ume, a plum blossom pattern. Although I grew up seeing my family crest on my mother's traditional kimono, I had never been interested in the meaning and origin of the crest

Learning to knit at fifty under the guidance of a skilled weaver in our community group, I've woven numerous scarves for my family, bridging the distance to my cherished faraway home. *Awakening Essence*, 2020

until this point. I learned that Sugawara no Michizane, a ninth-century Japanese poet, had been deified as Tenjin, god of poetry, calligraphy and scholarship. He loved plum trees, and after his deification, shrines dedicated to him used plum blossoms as a crest. I remembered the old plum tree in my grandparents' garden which gave us flowers and plums year after year, though its trunk was hollowed out into the shape of a canoe. My family Ume crest finally meant something to me.

To enhance the co-creation process of WOW, I added incentives by co-producing exhibitions at the University of British Columbia's student hub NEST, the Richmond Art Gallery and the Roundhouse Community Centre. Making everyone a stakeholder kept us engaged. As we prepared for exhibitions, many weavers visited my house, needles and thread in hand, to attach the woven squares to large, white, handmade frames. We put on music, shared personal histories and, through the window, watched a family of raccoons. We were transfixed, and we invented stories for the graceful creatures. Our preteen youth joined in, and friends and neighbours came to help us build weaving looms from scratch. Subsequently, we mounted exhibitions and created a print art catalogue.

The WOW project gave art a two-fold significance for me. In one sense, I saw it as harnessing intuition and artistic skill to express one's aesthetic insights to others. But I also saw it as a means of initiating co-creation, a way of tapping into the collective power of the community. There was an immediacy to the communal process of co-creating a blanket that was delightful. As Rainer Maria Rilke reveals in *Letters on Life*, the seed of future creation may arise at any moment. We need only to "summon it to visibility."[3] Co-creation is one means of making that future increasingly visible.

SIMON FRASER UNIVERSITY

In late May of 2019, I jumped again. It started with a short email to the acting director of Simon Fraser University's (SFU) Liberal Arts and 55+ Program. My email was abrupt, but I had nothing to lose. I had never done any teaching other than as a graduate assistant during my PhD studies and I was shy, but I became excited when I discovered the 55+ Program in SFU's continuing studies' catalogue.

I liked the diversity of topics and the instructors' varied backgrounds, but it seemed that most of the courses were traditionally top-down or lecture based, geared more toward knowledge acquisition than problem solving or research. *Perhaps that's what most seniors were comfortable with*, I assumed. But I began asking myself, *Wouldn't seniors be looking to pass on their life stories and skills to younger generations?* Coming from Japan, I naturally assumed that seniors were happier and healthier if they were fully integrated and appreciated in the community. This once again brought to mind the concept of *ikigai*—a reason for being.

Without having any information about the motivations of their student body, I was toying with the idea of proposing an experiment to the coordinators of the 55+ Program: What if I could bring something new to the program where seniors undertook art-based projects of their own? Would it help cultivate the demand and supply of senior mentors? Would it add meaning to anyone's life?

Every year since starting VACS, I had successfully applied for federal funding annually, including from the New Horizons for Seniors Program. One of VACS's mandates was to promote civic engagement among seniors and encourage their mentorship of younger community members. We were always tapping into the same cohort of local seniors who were willing, out of altruism and friendship, and healthy enough to mentor youth or co-create with them. I wanted to reach a different cohort of untapped or self-marginalized seniors who were missing such opportunities, so I took a chance. The acting director replied right away. We arranged a meeting two weeks from our initial contact.

The acting director and program coordinator were waiting for me, smiling broadly in a sun-filled bullpen office at Harbour Centre. I began describing my proposal for an active-learning course to provoke personal inquiry, access acquired wisdom and develop co-creating skills in the arts. As I had not yet named my "transdisciplinary" course, it was challenging to pitch my ideas in ways that they could understand. It became an immensely intriguing first conversation. I was impressed by how curious, respectful and open minded they were.

As soon as I returned from the meeting, I skyped my mother in Japan. She was in the final stages of stomach cancer and in palliative care in the hospital. I told her about my afternoon at Harbour Centre. She was so happy to hear about my adventure, and I could hear her summoning all her energy to be fully present for me.

"Mom, you used to say to me, 'If you don't enter the tiger's den, how will you get the tiger's cub?' That's what I felt like today. How is your pain?"

We talked for about thirty minutes. My eyes were watery. My mother was, in many ways, my inspiration for my work with seniors. Even in the difficult stage she was in, she was always sharing her wisdom with others.

Two weeks later, I received the official offer to teach a Liberal Arts and 55+ Program course in the spring semester of 2020. My mind started immediately racing. Spring 2020: another eight or nine months in the future. I could hardly contain my excitement—and nervousness. I had found my *ikigai*.

Relational Aesthetics

I live in West Southlands, a small subdivision of the larger neighbourhood Southlands. West Southlands has only three hundred households and is bordered by Southwest Marine Drive, the north arm of the Fraser River, Collingwood Street and the Musqueam reserve community. In the fall of 2022, I found a notice for the annual general meeting (AGM) of the West Southlands Residents Association (WSRA) in my mailbox. I hadn't heard about them before. I was grateful for—and curious about—these diligent neighbours who hand-delivered notices, remembering the *kairan ban*, a circulating community clipboard which most Japanese towns still use as a neighbourhood communication system. I decided to attend the AGM.

I met many kindred spirits there. I discovered that two of the WSRA's top priorities were protecting local biodiversity and building climate resilience. Before I knew it, I had joined the group and volunteered to help design their website, though I am no expert on website design. I wanted to help somehow, and they needed a website. I was moved by their commitment to make our area more hospitable for our non-human neighbours.

Spirited neighbours spontaneously gathering to discuss natural ecosystems and wildlife at risk—it was a performance piece. How could we visually convey this spirit through a website? This was my challenge. My experience making the website with my new WSRA friends was transformative; we were turning everything into art. And by that, I mean "relational" art. The French curator and critic Nicolas Bourriaud coined the phrase "relational aesthetics" in his 1998 book of the same name. He defined relational art as making art based on, or inspired by, human relationships and their social contexts. In a sense, the WSRA's AGM was, for me, a work of relational art.

How could I show the power of relational aesthetics to other people? Is a sense of place a *reception* that one receives, or is it an individual's *creation*? Could viewers interpret the website as relational art? Could a website provoke new aesthetic experiences in viewers that would inspire them to get involved with the WSRA?

One of the ways I attempted to achieve this was by inviting my neighbour Steve Hodder to share his photographs on the website. One Christmas, he mailed Christmas cards to his friends and neighbours and included a photograph of a snow-covered creek in West Southlands. While I recognized the location, I was mesmerized by the beauty. How could our neighbourhood look so iconic? I sensed his process of reflection. Even though appreciation can sometimes feel passive when compared to making art, it is still a creative act—a construction of meaning that reveals ordinary life in an extraordinary way. Steve's photographs are an invitation to participate in the act of seeing the community differently, and I think the healthiest response to contemporary society's alienation and isolation is to evoke a participatory sense of local community.

There are few experiences more meaningful than being guided by the wisdom of one's neighbours, especially our non-human neighbours. One third of the world's great blue herons live around the Salish Sea, and the Southlands' riverbanks are one of the vital foraging spots for these elegant birds, as the estuarine and freshwater marshes are rich in nutrients. I often spot them in my neighbourhood, always standing peacefully alone. Because the adults take up solitary lives, I feel a special kinship with them. Standing motionless, as if performing relational art, the great blue heron reveals the abundance of life in intertidal spaces with patience and grace. What do these intertidal spaces mean to me? Living in West Southlands is like standing in an intertidal zone, literally and figuratively. I notice—and thus create—the wild variety of pullulating life in these waters, myself and my relationships included.

I took the liberty of making it possible for people to submit their own artwork on the WSRA website, and one day I decided to submit my own watercolour rendition of a bank along the Fraser River. The painting embraces the *wabi-sabi* philosophy—an aesthetics of simplicity, imperfection and withered things—and celebrates the incomplete in everything. Rather than hiding our own receptions and expressions

Glimpse of the Fraser River bank from West Southlands, my beloved neighbour-hood. *Autumn Reflections, 2021*

because they seem incomplete and imperfect, we can instead see them as creations of nature—much as a bright red maple leaf might land on the green grass by our feet, revealing a colourful spectacle of which we are an essential part.

Expanding Ikigai

An email from a new acquaintance arrived out of the blue, asking if I would be interested in trying a yoga movement with her. This woman offered to travel to my home. How delightful and kind. She is a cognitive scientist, a professionally trained bassoonist, an educator and a seasoned weaver who joined WOW thanks to a mutual friend who connected us. On top of her impressive credentials and artistic talents, she is a long-time yoga practitioner for herself. What could she not do? Coincidentally, we were the same age, and each had a teenage child.

"YES, I am interested! I am free tomorrow!" I immediately responded, feeling ecstatic. The timing of her email was exquisite. It was

The ethereal glow that envelops the Fraser River bank in the tranquil moments after sunset. *Winter Reflections, 2021*

two years into the COVID-19 pandemic, and for the first time throughout this period, I was feeling that my "social muscles" had atrophied. I had become too lazy to go out with friends for fun and instead stayed home, absorbed in my work. It felt like some of my neurons used during social engagement were retracting, but her email was an electric signal, figuratively—and probably literally, reconnecting dusty neural pathways.

She likely sensed my enthusiasm when I saw her a few weeks earlier. I had invited her to participate in my grant application. I was seeking funding so I could design a disabled-inclusive exercise program through VACS to replace those currently available, which were semi-segregated classes that treated physical ability as a binary state: one was either disabled or abled, when disability is better understood as on a continuum. I felt frustrated by the existing classes, despite the many well-thought-out fitness programs available. I was proposing a more inclusive community practice that would transcend boundaries between abled and disabled. I had asked her what these inclusive methods might look like in real life and about the viability of my proposal. In my conversation with her, I also revealed my embarrassment at my inability to move most parts of my body in the ways I wanted, let alone re-experience the graceful ballet movement I enjoyed when I was young.

The day after she sent the email, she showed up at my door with her guitar. She looked very comfortable in her own skin, sporting a tweed trapper's hat, a red-and-black-plaid scarf, her own hand-knitted grey vest, blue jeans and black boots. Each piece had its own personality. Most of all, her eyes were sparkling.

"Are you ready?" This was the moment of truth.

I hid my embarrassment under my big smile. "Yes!" I replied.

We sat in my quiet living room. She started a gentle breathing movement, which I first watched and then imitated in unison with her. She then started to play dreamy chords on her guitar while I continued the breathing exercise. I closed my eyes to avoid eye contact, as that would have made me self-conscious. Her music helped me relax. I was no longer self-conscious. She began to seem angelic, and I was mesmerized. There were eight movement sequences in total, in gentle progression, and there was meaning attached to each nuanced sequence. I absorbed her fluid movements, which she performed in perfect tempo, as if she were hearing music that was inaudible to me. She was a trained musician, after all. I was amazed by how she transformed simple yoga into an art form as graceful as what my modern ballet teacher used to teach when I was young.

Suddenly, the image of my deceased mother hula dancing entered my mind. She would explain how hula was language-driven and a way of telling stories while moving her whole body, from her fingertips to her eyes. I found myself wanting to master the eight movement sequences, seduced by their grace and meaning.

After an hour-long session, we shared lunch and talked for a couple of hours.

"I found it very interesting that you were enticed to practise because of the artistry," she said.

"Yes. It was not about doing it right physically as an exercise. If that had been the case, I would have lost interest. But I was drawn to the freedom of expression embedded in each movement, like a dance. You moved so gracefully. I felt there was an ultimate goal, which was that I could perform the movement as a way of expressing how I felt."

Ah *hah*! At that moment, we both realized what inclusive methods might look like in real life. It was about creating a space for free kinetic expression, unified—not constrained—by a shared rhythm and common form. That comprised both the means and goals of the community program we wanted to create. If we could harness free artistic expression in our exercise method, that could allow the community to form, develop and evolve.

I was immensely grateful. Even without a clear plan, we had somehow solved the puzzle by doing things together and then reflecting together. We were finding a shared sense of purpose, a community-forming *ikigai*.

SUBLIME CONNECTION

I was waiting for a traffic light to turn green at an intersection in my neighbourhood when a well-dressed, soft-spoken gentleman asked me, in Japanese, "Excuse me. Are you Japanese?" He slightly bowed. His face looked familiar.

"*Hai*," I confirmed, in the same language. I had known he was Japanese before he spoke.

"My wife and I recently went foraging for bracken fiddleheads from the woods nearby. If you like, we could bring you some," said Mr. Ogawa.

As soon as I heard "bracken fiddleheads" in Japanese I felt a surge of nostalgia. When was the last time I ate them? Twenty years ago? I used to go to Mount Aso with my family to forage for fiddleheads in the spring, and then my grandma would cook them for us.

"Thank you so much—but I'm afraid I don't know how to cook fiddleheads."

"No problem. We will cook them and bring them to you."

The following day, Mr. and Mrs. Ogawa visited my house with a large bento box beautifully wrapped in a Japanese *furoshiki* cloth. Mrs. Ogawa, like a lily flower, emitted a clean, feminine presence that I found enchanting. She transported me back to Japan. And—there they were! The elegant, subtly fragrant fiddleheads lit my appetite and my memory. We had a joyful afternoon drinking tea and making friends. They lived only two minutes from Maya and me. It was May 2011. There were cherry blossoms outside.

The Ogawas entered our lives. They often came to the AIR Salon, bringing Mrs. Ogawa's potlucks, instantly popular and the first to disappear.

A spontaneous sketch capturing the cherished faces of our weaving community, Weaving Our Way (WOW), amidst the challenges of the COVID pandemic.

Mrs. Ogawa had studied fashion in Japan, and one day she asked seven-year-old Maya what she wanted to be for Halloween.

"Ninja!" Maya said.

Mrs. Ogawa brought a measuring stick, scissors, sewing machine and textiles to make a ninja costume in collaboration with Maya, whom she taught to use the sewing machine.

In the spring of 2017, I received an email from a Ms. Paula Sawadsky, who was working for the producer of some films to be displayed at the Royal BC Museum in Victoria. She invited me to submit photos for the film and exhibition titled *Family: Bonds and Belonging*. She was particularly interested in "intergenerational teaching," and Mr. and Mrs. Ogawa's faces rose in my mind, their quiet, open-handed generosity spreading like concentric rings. We were a family.

The producers chose one photograph for the archival film out of the collection I sent. Mrs. Ogawa is seen teaching Maya how to present food on a plate during the preparation of a full-course, Japanese-themed community dinner we had organized, showing the art of Japanese hosting. Maya's intense concentration invests the otherwise-still image with vibrant movement.

SALT SPRING ISLAND

July 2013

"We can take you and Maya to Salt Spring Island!" said my friend Robin, a registered forester. His young forestry intern, Cassandra, who helped me start my front yard vegetable garden, was planning to spend her summer on Salt Spring working at the Harbour House Hotel's organic farm. Cassandra and Robin researched how to bring me and Maya safely there, and how to keep us entertained. They were so caring that I was already there in spirit, though I could not imagine how we would travel to a rural environment with my wheelchair and eight-year-old Maya.

I was newly separated from my husband, and the fifty-fifty custody was taxing. Being a single mother in a wheelchair was something I had not planned. While I was struggling to adapt, I had given up the idea of travelling with my eight-year-old. It seemed impossible. Robin sensed my resignation, a very Japanese way of coping. My friends designed the travelling arrangements in concert. The impossible mission became a grand plan with the addition of two more guardian angels, Lilia and Gabriel, my muses and free-spirit friends. So, the five of us, of different ages, shapes and backgrounds, embarked on a three-day adventure.

It was exuberant and salubrious. I had four of my close friends by my side, slowing their paces to my speed, sharing beautiful vistas from my eye level. We toured a lavender farm, ate at lively local restaurants and drove around the island in my wheelchair-accessible van.

Then, we travelled to Cusheon Lake. The island was dense with lakes and beaches. I had packed Maya's bathing suits and towels in our travel bags, as Lilia and Cassandra were keen on swimming. While reaching for Maya's towel, I noticed that Lilia and Maya, who were in the back seat, were alive with mischievous smiles.

"We have a surprise for you," said Lilia. She handed me a small piece of fabric. "It's my extra bikini! We want you to swim with us!"

"Wait, what!?" I was astonished. I was planning to watch everyone else swim, from wherever I could perch my wheelchair, and enjoy the view.

Maya was grinning at me now, too, and Gabriel said, "Yap! I'm on it! I'll stay with you the whole time, so no worries, Keiko!" Everyone knew the secret plan except for me. How could I say no, now that my friends had put so much work and thought into this?

I had never worn a bikini in my life, and I was scared of the lake's murky bottom and felt intensely vulnerable. But I especially did not want to disappoint Maya. I somehow managed to change into the bikini. Though Gabriel was young and athletic, I was not sure he could really carry me... and what if the bikini fell off in the water? This was completely new terrain.

With my arms around his neck, Gabriel gently carried me to the lake like a princess. "Ready?"

The lake water felt soft, like a silk scarf, and was surprisingly warm and pristine. It gently swayed with its own aqueous music. I saw large birds in the distant air returning to the water, sliding on their bellies. I felt free, and Gabriel was reassuring. I forgot all fear of the lake. Maya and Lilia were far away. I knew Maya was a good swimmer but had never imagined her swimming in a vast, deep lake.

"Bobbing—ready? I'll count to three. One. Two. Three!" He ducked.

I held my breath. In the water, I felt the sensation of bubbles all around my bare skin. We did a lot of bobbing.

"Let's swim over there. Hold me tight!" I was on his back, holding onto his neck. We were like two turtles piling on top of each other. In the water, my body moved smoothly and flexibly with no restriction—total freedom in nature. I even drank a little lake water by accident. How tasty!

The next day, we went to the beach. Except for Robin, we all went into the ocean despite the overcast morning. The ocean water was cold and rough with the push and pull from the strong current and had a distinct salt smell. It was not the calm-looking ocean it had seemed from a distance; being inside the current gave me a new perspective. Gabriel and I immersed ourselves to our waists, bodies resting on shallow tidal gravel. Even though we were just sitting, we were moving with the current like seaweed. He held me tight from the back and I was grabbing his thighs to balance; otherwise, I would have floated away like a leaf. Maya and Lilia were again far away, swimming. I was a bit worried, but they had a great time and returned full of energy. Everyone was free in nature. The photos Robin took of the four of us rendered us as tiny dots merging into the seascape. We returned to Vancouver with strong memories and stronger friendships.

Seven years later, I was painting my memories of Salt Spring Island in watercolours. Bodily memories. Water seems to touch the deepest

As the ocean waves caress our feet, Gabriel tenderly lifts me, carrying me into their embrace, while Maya stands captivated from afar, witnessing the mesmerizing spectacle unfold. *Summer, 2013*

part of me, especially flowing water. I often wonder whether my sudden fascination with watercolours came from my childhood memories of Kumamoto water or if it was connected to the embodied feeling of water supporting my weight that I felt on Salt Spring. Maybe both.

Working with Nature

"She creates new forms without end: what exists now, never was before; what was, comes not again; all is new and yet always the old." —Goethe, *Maxims and Reflections,* 1906[4]

I began experimenting with watercolour painting at the end of 2019. I set up a little station at home and begun painting some simple leaves, trees and skies. Throughout this process, I learned how our perceptions form our reality, and that we could train our perceptions. I'd begun noticing how my powers of observation had sharpened. I gradually became aware that the blue-coloured pigments I was using were not adequate for capturing the blue of the sky. The sky had grey in it, and purple, and warm yellow too. The shadow on the ground was not black; rather, it was purple, or cool blue, or other colours depending on the environment in which the shadow falls. When I was observing like that, trying to capture the reality of the outside world, I also felt that I was part of it, and that there were infinite possible realities waiting to be discovered.

So, I was excited when, in the summer of 2020, I found out about a group of community members who had organized a *plein-air* painting session at Jericho Beach Park, one of the most beautiful parks in Vancouver. It was special to me because I spent a lot of time there when my daughter was small. As a novice watercolourist and new to *plein-air* painting, I was initially eager, but soon found myself feeling very frustrated. I felt like a snail slowly drawing back into its shell as my confidence sank. I managed to stay to the end of the session, but to my mind my painting was an illustrated admission of defeat.

I had not bothered to rehearse at home, so I was unprepared for the practical challenges, including the limited working space: my lap. I had to hold the brushes and palette in my hands while keeping my paper and water container on my lap. On top of that, I forgot to bring a cloth to wipe the palette, so soon I only had muddy colours to work with. In the foreground, there were flocks of free-ranging Canada geese grazing in the grass and approaching my setup. But most of all, I was simply overwhelmed with the complexity of the information—the colours, shapes and movements—of nature that I wanted to capture. The more I noticed the vivid details, which changed by the second, the more unfocussed I became, and the more I was distracted by the heat. The session was held in mid-afternoon in the last stretch of summer; it was very muggy. I was embarrassed that I had assumed that the landscape owed me something. *How did I get the idea that it should look a certain way, when it was constantly changing and evolving, just as I am?* My first *plein-air* painting was memorably miserable.

Emily Carr writes, "Outdoor study was as different from studio study as eating is from drinking.... Sketching outdoors was a fluid process, half-looking, half-dreaming, awaiting invitation from the spirit of the subject to 'come, meet me halfway.' Outdoor sketching was as much longing as labour."[5] My first session was indeed laborious—that much was true. But Goethe's description of nature got me thinking: "We live in the midst of her and are strangers. She speaks to us unceasingly

Exploring *plein-air* painting along a nearby forest trail unveiled invaluable lessons that elude studio settings: the varying drying speeds, ever-shifting lighting, and the symphony of nature's melodies—a holistic sensory journey! *Musqueam Park Trail*, 2021

and betrays not her secret. We are always influencing her and yet can do her no violence."[6] I was beginning to understand. *Plein-air* painting was a discipline dependent upon the constantly fluctuating natural light and conditions. Capturing and executing what we saw was only part of the whole: one's attitude and emotions mattered. My labour, eye movements and dexterity with the material must be tuned to nature, and at the same time free to dance with her.

I re-engaged with my attempt at *plein-air* painting the following summer. I decided to master it through a kind of heuristic evolution: using repetitive practice and observation, taking advantage of the mistakes that turned out to be good things and remembering not to repeat the failures. I formed a *plein-air* watercolour painting group with a small number of like-minded people as a way to keep myself moving forward. Five women of all ages and backgrounds—Beth, Yvonne, Deighen, Inanna and Doloris—joined me in this experiment. We initially planned to meet for two hours in the park, but when I received funding from

Neighbourhood Small Grants (NSG), a community-building grant program created by the Vancouver Foundation, we extended the two-hour session to five hours total. We spent those additional three hours in my front yard, which we had catered. I loved the spontaneity and serendipity of how it developed. There was always much laughter. As the saying goes, "Three women (and a goose) make a market." Our process is fluid, delicate and dynamic, like watercolours.

I committed myself to *plein-air* watercolour painting that summer—to the way it enhances my visual memory and attention to the laws of nature, which is worthy of intense study. As Emily Carr would say, "Come, meet me halfway"! That was the whole spirit, and I know my grandfather would agree.

The Hidden Flower

I had met Leta Goldwynn twice at events I had organized to create a mini watercolour palette to encourage *plein-air* painting, but in the summer of 2021, she invited me to her own workshop, part of her NSG project of handmaking mini palettes for watercolours. How like-minded! I was hungry for this kind of learning, but my initial enthusiasm waned when I found out I would get my second COVID-19 shot one day before her event. I was concerned about side effects. As usual, I was also thinking about wheelchair accessibility, including bathroom access and transportation, though she had said that her backyard was accessible and had a covered gazebo. I chickened out at the last minute.

Then she sent an email. "Please let me come visit you." I was deeply moved. I felt not only her special sensitivity to my circumstances, but also a certain poetic quality that I don't normally find in everyday interactions. She could have just offered me some art materials to come pick up, or simply said, "Please join us next time." Instead, she surprised me.

The following rainy Sunday afternoon, she came to my home with a box full of art supplies. As soon as she arrived, I put the kettle on so we could enjoy each other's company over coffee and cakes I had prepared. Interestingly, we both came from sophisticated tea cultures—Japanese and Irish—and enjoyed sharing cross-cultural observations regarding Vancouver hospitality. I was intrigued by her way of making mini palettes out of polymer clay, a material I did not know about! Using our fingers to create our ideal mini palette was like playing with playdough and was fun and calming. We put our newly sculpted palettes in the oven to bake at 275°F (130°C) for thirty minutes to finish. And *voilà*! I was mesmerized by the buff-coloured and smoothly surfaced square. After she left, a glow lingered for days.

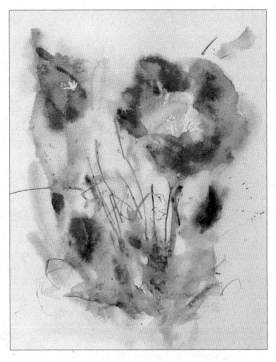

Unveiling the tender and delicate expression of hidden flowers within. *Hidden Flowers,* 2021

The whole episode reminded me of the famous aphorism concerning "secrecy" by Zeami Motokiyo, a Japanese aesthetician and co-founder of the classical Noh theatre born in the fourteenth century, who explained his aesthetic principles in the book *Fūshikaden* (風姿花伝), which translates to *The Transmission of the Flower Through (a Mastery of) the Forms.* He elaborates on what he means by "secrecy" in art using images of nature as a repeated metaphor: "What is hidden will become the flower. What is not hidden cannot become the flower." [7] He then explains the importance of secrecy and indirection for audiences. He says that when you start by saying you will show something unusual (*mezurashiki*), the audience doesn't get too surprised because they expect it, but if you suddenly show something unusual without telling them in advance, they will be surprised and excited. Giving people unexpected emotions—that is what Zeami's concept of the "flower" is. The hidden thing itself is not that important, but something is created by hiding it.

Ah *hah*! That explained my excitement that afternoon with Leta. While difficult to express, we all know that wondrous feeling that blooms when least expected. The flower can be communicated to other people. My experience with Leta was Zeami's hidden flower. It was not spectacular or obvious; rather, it was the secret transmission of elegance, grace and enlightenment.

My Uncle's Teacup

Sipping green tea, my uncle asked, "Keiko-chan, why do you think we don't drink coffee from these Japanese teacups? And why do we never drink green tea out of a coffee mug?"

We were sitting around a *chabudai*, a low dining table, in my grandparents' living room. I was ten years old and my uncle—my mother's younger brother—must have been thirty. He was a *freeter*, an adult no longer a student and without full-time employment. With medium-long hair and large, black-framed glasses, he still looked like a student. My mother once told me that he had joined the student movement when he was in university and was blacklisted because of his activism. It was hush-hush, as though being on the red list was a crime. I was on his side and felt protective.

My uncle, who was living at my grandparents' house, was like my big brother. I remember him reading thick books, playing guitar and singing, oil painting like my grandfather, and smoking cigarettes while sketching. He left his butts in a flower-shaped ashtray decorated with a grey-glazed pattern—a distinct feature of Kirishima ware—from my grandfather's collection. Occasionally, his siblings, mostly my mother, nagged him to "Get your act together and find a job!" On the other hand, his parents, my grandparents, hardly said anything critical and always spoke to him (and everyone) lovingly and gently. As a child, I adored him, as he not only helped me with my arts and crafts homework but also spoke in riddles, unlike other family members who acted more grownup. I felt as though the flow of time stopped at my grandparents' house.

"Umm... because... it would taste weird?" I answered. I held the teacup in both hands and gulped the lukewarm tea down.

"Hmmm, you think it would taste weird." he smiled.

"Oh, I know, I know! We can hold a teacup like this," I demonstrated, "because green tea is never too hot to hold. But coffee is hotter, so we need the handle," I added, as if I finally found the answer.

At around ten years old, I had started drinking instant coffee, adding a spoonful of powdered creamer, which was my secret snack back then. While mixing the hot water, coffee and creamer, I was often mesmerized by the white froth floating on top in a whirl. I would breathe in the tantalizing scent from my big coffee mug. As a child, making and drinking my own cup of coffee made me feel independent.

I don't remember how our conversation went from there, but I vividly remember his seemingly random question. The rest of my extended family never expressed doubts about Japanese norms and customs nor had time to ponder alternatives. After living in North America for over two decades, I rarely use my small Japanese teacups, which are now at the back of the kitchen cupboard. The only time I use them is when I have a guest to impress.

I remember drinking green tea with my beloved grandmother. She always asked, "Keiko-chan, can I pour you more tea?" If my tea was cold, she never bothered to empty the cup, but would pour warm, fresh tea into my cup. Chatting and laughing, we held the teacups in our hands and felt the warmth of the tea... or perhaps we were feeling the warmth of each other's hands. *Te no nukumori*—the warmth of the teacup is like the warmth of a human hand. My grandmother passed away long ago, but I still remember the warmth of her dry, chapped hands—and herein lies the answer to my uncle's question, asked when I was ten years old in 1978.

YŪGEN

Zeami Motokiyo was fond of the concept *yūgen* (幽玄), "the beauty of gentle grace," one of the most elegant and subtle concepts in Japanese culture. Over the centuries, *yūgen* has expanded from the supernatural to the earthly, from the mystic to the human. Even for Japanese, the elusive idea of *yūgen* is hard to articulate, which is part of the idea. It is a deep-rooted grace and subtlety.

I developed my grasp of *yūgen,* and love of nature, throughout my childhood in Japan, but as an immigrant, I am still rediscovering the culture of my youth and reshaping my Japanese identity in a Canadian context. And since I moved to Canada—the first country to formally establish a "multiculturalism" policy—I have been curious about how multiculturalism is changing. The ideal cultural practice in Canada would be to not enforce a single, standard culture, but to establish and maintain mutually respectful relationships between cultures within a context of tolerance and sharing. But my most pressing question, the one I've been pondering for a long time, is how we come to identify with *and* distinguish ourselves from our interconnected communities. To understand myself and be whole, I must embrace my Japanese sensibilities, many learned from my family, including the most ineffable.

LESSONS FROM MY GRANDFATHER

My grandfather Konosuke Masuda taught me—through spoken words as well as through his character and actions—to find and share inspiration. When I turned fifty, I wondered how I could cultivate energy and harmony in later life and what I needed to learn. Curious about his construction of a beautiful, extensive worldview, I rediscovered his practices, which turned out to be just what I needed.

My grandfather was a banker by trade, a lone wolf when he was young and a bookworm throughout his life. He was a meticulous note

During my childhood, I often spent time wandering through nature's enchanting labyrinth on Mt. Aso. One vivid memory that lingers is the captivating transformation of the pampas grass, as it turned into a gentle golden meadow, dancing with the distant insects' calling as autumn unfolded. *Feeling Yūgen*, 2021

taker and kept a pen and a small sketchbook in his shirt pocket. Beginning in his early fifties, he grew increasingly passionate about his hobbies, such as *plein-air* painting, reading, writing, Bonsai, photography, fishing, the Japanese board game Go, and travelling. As is customary of *plein-air* painters, he always painted places, objects and people exactly as he found them. I vividly remember his wooden, leather-handled painting briefcase that travelled with him everywhere. He left over a thousand oil and watercolour paintings, countless poems and sketches and a self-published memoir that documents his personal experiences of World War II, and how strongly he condemned that unjustifiable war.

I was always around my grandfather, whether he was doing his *plein-air* painting or sitting in his quiet study, heavy with oil paint fumes. I never really understood the world he created until I began to learn how to paint as an adult; it was not until then that I understood that within his art was a representation of the world as he saw and understood it. Moreover, through my own act of painting, I was beginning to discover and share a similar sort of care, awe, humility and gentleness that shaped his late-life learning.

He observed the world with inner contentment. At every moment, he was observing the changing landscapes—not only as an artist, but also as a naturalist. Without exaggerating, he spent most of his free time in nature, especially in his splendid garden that attracted birds and dragonflies. He wrote this poem at age seventy-seven (my translation):

欲もかれ（枯）　　自然や花に　喜びを
絵筆とるとき　新たな命　（平成5年2月）

> Though I have lost my desires,
> I still find joy in nature and flowers.
> When I hold my paint brush,
> I renew the excitement of life. (February 1993)

One of his oil paintings depicts his sun-filled atelier by the garden, which he designed and maintained with constant care on his hands and knees. This painting, painted perhaps in February, shows the big old plum tree with white plum blossoms, about which he often wrote poems. That tree produced many plums year after year, which my grandmother made into Japanese salted plum, my favourite food. Just thinking about it makes my mouth water! The yellow-flowered tree—weeping forsythia—in the distance emits intense fragrance in my memory.

In the painting, the wooden armchair with soft upholstery is at his desk and I feel his corporeal presence in it, as if the chair represented his warm, humble character. The positioning of the chair, slightly removed from and perpendicular to the desk, surrounded by his garden through the large widows, conveys his sense of readiness, his studious nature and his deep love of the natural world. On the desk are the simplest, most ordinary objects—pens, paint brushes, notebooks, books, flowers, a radio, a teacup and a work-in-progress canvas of Mount Aso, the subject he painted the most—which reveal so many memories as I look at them. All these objects, his things, represent his state of mind. I love how he used the weight of whiteness to render the morning sunlight hitting half of the desk surface, echoing the intense colour of the robust plum blossoms outdoors. This gives the painting not only visual balance but also a certain significance—a feeling of having arrived at a place of freedom, awe and regenerative energy, like the spring season.

His garden was my childhood playground. I used to sit at the edge

The image of Mt. Aso in spring evokes cherished memories from the depths of my mind. *Mt. Aso Memories, (Version 2)*, 2021

of the pond for hours, enjoying the colourful koi. We used to clean the pond every summer, which was a whole-day family event involving emptying the water and scrubbing and removing the accumulated moss at the bottom and sides of the pond. As a child, the highlight was catching the large koi, about five or six of them at least, with a landing net in order to keep them in a large bucket while we cleaned. That was a big deal for me. I can still recall the sensation of the agile, slippery koi moving in my hands.

Another painting of his garden depicts the arrival of autumn with bright foliage. The pond looks mysterious: there is no reflection of the foliage, no shadow of koi under the surface of the deep-blue water and among the large rocks. But the autumn leaves are saturated in the golden, scarlet and brown colours of the koi I used to play with. Did he paint the autumn garden in the colours of his treasured koi? Did he forget to paint them? I am convinced that his emotional connection to the koi never left him, despite their absence in the painting and even once they passed on.

The Higo Tsubaki, my beloved flowers, known as the city emblem of Kumamoto, bloomed abundantly in my grandfather's cherished garden. *Grandfather's Tsubaki, 2021*

To what extent did Konosuke's artistic practices endow him with the strength to overcome his natural fragility, up to the moment of his death? This question haunts me now. He died of gastric cancer when he was eighty-four, five years after his gastrectomy. In the hospital, he continued to paint, write poetry and take notes. On the morning of his surgery, he wrote:

手術を前に　年令（よわい）八十　いろいろあるが
生きざまん　己を通して　我れ悔いなし
（平成七年６月５日）

Right before my surgery, nearly there, my eight-year-old mark. Even though I am battling illness and the spread of death before me, I am living life intensely through all my senses. I have no regrets. (June 5, 1995)

His physical health went into a slow decline after his cancer diagnosis. I started feeling guilty about my grandparents, whom I loved most in the world yet left behind when I moved to New York, just as he was facing this mortal ordeal. I was afraid to think that I might have been so self-absorbed that I abandoned those close relationships, but when I found this poem, which captured his moment of frailty, I felt consoled.

I found the delicacy of this next poem tricky to translate, and some of its meaning may escape translation. I had an extensive phone discussion about its meaning with my uncle (one of Konosuke's sons). The literal translation would be: "Being old, I am ashamed of becoming agitated and distracted. One day, me too... I feel so sad." My grandfather did not state specifically what he was agitated and anxious about or distracted from. Was it death, or something else? My grandfather was practising Zen and must have seen death as a natural part of life, so it was unlikely that he was disturbed by it. He was always conscious and eager to live fully and freely. Accordingly, I interpreted the poem as follows:

老いぬれば　心乱れて　みぐるしく
やがて我もと　思えばかなし（平成八年2月）

I am anxious about losing control and freedom (to create)
as I grow frail. One day, I too, might lose human dignity, and
I feel sad when I think about it. (February 1996)

Konosuke did not stop what he loved to do most—*plein-air* painting—even as he grew older. Nature seemed to have a positive effect on his emotional state. In 1996, he wrote:

水ぬるみ　菜の花も咲く　江津湖にて
スケッチなどして　今年も遊ぶ（平成八年3月30日）

Water has been lukewarm, and the canola plant is flowering.

I am sketching at Ezuko Lake. Let's play this year as well.
(March 30, 1996)

石佛は　やさしくおわす　吾が命
あと幾日や　絵がく生きがい（平成八年9月19日）

> The sculpted stone Buddha (in a garden) is looking at me kindly, compassionately. How many more days will I live? Being able to paint feeds my spirit to live. (September 19, 1996)

I continue to be astonished not only by his forbearance and determination to create, leaving no room for despair, but also by his unfailing sense of awe and wonder, even when he was struggling with cancer. His artistic practice trained his mind and body to respond with reverence to the world around him. Although he regularly painted his face throughout his life, his poignant self-portrait that year touches me deeply. Though it may seem cliché, I bear witness to his inner transformation through painting and poetry, and I affirm that our cognition is not confined to the mind but is also determined by bodily experiences of the physical world. His close attention and fascination to nature and his devotion to painting the world he observed may in turn have allowed him to look at himself as part of nature.

Konosuke was gentle, kind, patient and, most of all, a diligent student of spiritual pursuits. In late life, he often recited the word *mushin* (無心), a state of mind free from illusion. He did not bother anyone about the details of his sufferings; instead, he consciously sought to experience a sense of peaceful emptiness by exposing himself to nature and all living things.

When he was eighty-one and battling advanced cancer, Konosuke painted an almost-abstract, figurative interpretation of the active Nakadake Crater in Mount Aso in watercolours. Toward the end of his life, his medium shifted from oil to watercolours, as oil painting takes more time to complete, and his compositions became more abstract and simplified. The painting of the crater is one of his most moving paintings: The crater's vast space and the dynamic movement of smoke remind us of our constantly changing, diverse and complex reality, as well as our own impermanence. With this painting, he took me inside himself, as he, in turn, was inside the chaos of nature.

His lifelong *plein-air* practice helped him develop an enhanced visual memory and quick sketching skills, because the light and the natural environmental conditions are unstable; but I wonder if *plein-air* also

A sincere homage to my cherished grandfather, Konosuke, whose canvas became a sanctuary for capturing the very soul of Mt. Aso. *The Legacy of Grandfather's Plein-Air*, 2019

prepared him to embrace the change that included his own imminent death. I imagine that his artwork and thinking evolved together, leading him to peaceful, noble self-transcendence.

Art in the Home

I grew up with the smell of Konosuke's oil paint, but my earliest memory of looking at art is of a reproduction of *The Gleaners* by Jean-François Millet (1857). It hung on the wall next to the bathroom of my grandparents' home, facing the main entrance. Theirs was a modest, traditional Japanese house. I vividly remember every tidy corner. The floors of the corridors and the main entrance were always shining as if they were wet, because my grandmother would wipe them with a damp cloth every day.

It was considered odd to hang Western art by the front door of a traditional Japanese house, but I did not know this as a child. The reason I remember the painting so well is that the contrast between light and dark created a special emotional tension for me. As a five year old, I was afraid of the dark, especially when walking alone to the bathroom at the end of that dark corridor. Sometimes I ran into a huge spider in the corner of the ceiling: every time I got close to the bathroom door, I looked up to see if there was a spider, which determined my walking speed and my heart rate. At the same time, I briefly looked at the dimly lit painting.

Installed on the wall under an incandescent light bulb, the painting glowed with soft, warm, sombre colours that blended into the glistening dark brown of the wooden floor. The beauty of the painting distracted me and eased my fear. I often stood there alone, mesmerized by how delicate and soft those women seemed, and yet how lifelike. The sculpted weight of the figures in the foreground were lit by the slanting light of the setting sun. The play of light and dark created the illusion of depth and carried the drama of the painting. I don't remember if I paid any attention to that painting in daylight, but when night fell it grew deeply engaging, glowing against my grandparents' bare corridor wall as if it had its own circadian rhythm. Initially, it calmed my fear of darkness; as I grew, it evolved into something more complex—a series of see-think-wonder moments. I feel my life would be different if I had not glanced at that painting every day.

Later, as an adult, I saw the original in the Musée d'Orsay and read about Millet. Although he was initially criticized for depicting rural poverty and class strife in nineteenth-century France, the skillful way he depicted the transient light on the landscape was a major influence on

During my childhood, I would always gaze at *The Gleaners* while passing through the corridor on my way to the bathroom. *Alone with The Gleaners*, 2021

the Impressionists. He also conveyed the dignity of rural workers, living so close to nature that they became sublime. This idea of finding the sublime in the commonplace is the spirit of *wabi-sabi*. Although I wish I could have had a conversation with my grandfather about why he liked *The Gleaners* so much that he hung it in the entrance hall, it must have stirred the hearts of my grandparents, who embraced modesty, labour, humility and nature. I wonder what my grandmother saw in the painting while she was wiping the floor on her hands and knees.

My grandmother, Tamiko, devoted her whole life to her family and endured many hardships during and after World War II. She raised five children, served her husband and mother-in-law with great pride and helped raise many grandchildren. The life of women in the early twentieth century was centred around caregiving, without, of course, any help from modern technology. I remember how her rough, cracked hands felt in mine. She always kept me from washing dishes, saying, "It will damage your beautiful, silky hands." I imagine that she must have taken solace seeing herself in those dignified, hard-working women in the painting.

I have, in my home in Vancouver, a replica of a Kitagawa Utamaro drawing in the *nikuhitsu-ga* (hand painted) *ukiyo-e* genre, which became popular among ordinary people during the Edo Period. *Ukiyo-e* originally implied hand-painted pictures that depicted everyday life, such as beautiful women engaged in leisurely pursuits. At the end of the seventeenth century, *ukiyo-e* began to be mass-produced because of the arrival and great affordability of woodblock printing. Many artists embraced the wide range of subject matter, including caricature that symbolically and humorously criticized the government. In 1799, the government began a campaign of censorship and seized art that was politically subversive. My grandfather was a collector of *ukiyo-e* reproductions, and he gave me a few when I left Kumamoto in 1976; my favourite, a triptych called *Abalone Divers* (Awabi tori) (ca. 1797–98), has travelled from Kumamoto to Tokyo to New York to (finally) Vancouver. The reproduction depicts women divers who plunge into the sea to harvest pearls—a traditional Japanese trade for women practised for over two thousand years. Half-naked, one working woman is breastfeeding a child while combing her still-wet, stringy black hair after a day of diving into the ocean. No time to rest.

Utamaro created many *ukiyo-e* drawings of this most natural and satisfying aspect of motherhood, which I find astonishingly beautiful and resonant.

I was a formula-fed baby because my mom was a working professional, but she also could not produce enough breast milk. Accordingly, I was ignorant about breastfeeding. My feelings about whether I would breastfeed or bottle-feed my future child were arbitrary. And yet, I am living proof that motherhood brings dramatic changes to the brain in women, because once I was pregnant I became determined to exclusively feed Maya breast milk for at least one full year. Plan A was to freeze my milk and hire a nanny, but Maya was stubborn and kept refusing the bottle. So, I switched to Plan B, which was to keep nursing, hire a nanny and bring both baby and nanny to the university. I still vividly remember how difficult it was to stay focussed during one seminar presentation once I saw the nanny out of the corner of my eye: she was bouncing Maya, who could not hold still any longer and was about to cry. I slowly but surely got better at nursing at work, just like those divers in Utamaro's drawing.

During Maya's first year, I kept gazing at the Utamaro drawing hanging in my study. In the modern world, public nursing was often frowned upon, depending on where you lived. There was no word for *breast milk* in the Edo period in Japan; they just called it *milk* because nursing was the only nutrition a newborn human could get. But nursing was more than nutrition: it promoted bonding and attachment between mother and baby, which played a critical role in a child's emotional development. Luckily, through much trial and error, I managed to exclusively breastfeed Maya for that first critical year and beyond, with the help of many kind people. And as a mother-in-training, I was not only guided by Utamaro's drawing; I also privately celebrated its authentic depiction of motherhood. I often giggled because Maya was doing the exact same thing as the child in the painting: touching and pinching his mother's other nipple while being nursed. How universal! I wish I could express my thanks to Utamaro, the eighteenth-century artist who drew nature as it was. Could he ever imagine that public nursing could become so controversial? Probably not.

As nursing became second nature, my feeling toward the painting evolved from wonder to contentment and comaraderie with all mothers, past, present and future. I look forward to the day my daughter can embrace this painting in her own way.

TASTING WITH YOUR EYES: MY GRANDMOTHER'S WISDOM

"The inside has to be white," said my beloved grandmother, Tamiko, when choosing a cup to serve me *sencha*—everyday green tea.

Tamiko used to routinely soak all the teacups in bleach to remove tea stains. In my youth, I used to wonder why she bothered. I had never really thought her effort had any meaning, other than expressing her habitually clean, hardworking nature. But the reasons she was so particular about the whiteness of the inside of a teacup were much more complex.

Sencha, if brewed correctly, is light in colour, transparent yellow or yellow-green. Delicate, young tea like *sencha* is judged by its colour to determine its level of freshness. It must be gently steeped. Thus, it is distinct from thick, frothy, bright green *matcha*, which is made by whipping finely ground tea powder. My grandmother, who drank somewhere between ten and fifteen small cups of tea a day throughout her life, could discern the taste of the tea even before tasting, just by observing the shade of green. I am no tea connoisseur, but I know my favourite colour of *sencha*, which comes in the first and second steep. By the third round, it loses its greenish colour (becoming too yellow), soothing aromas and sweet flavours. By the fourth round, it is no longer my cup of tea.

The effects of colour on taste and flavour identification have long been studied by cognitive neuroscientists, including not just the hue (red, green, blue, yellow) but also saturation and opacity. Because we look into the cup before drinking, our eyes send signals to our brain well before our taste buds and smell receptors engage. This can influence how we perceive the taste and flavour, and this is why my grandmother never served green tea in a stained cup or a cup whose interior was any colour other than white. For her, the pure white of the inside of a teacup was essential for experiencing the whole life course of green tea. Imagine how confused our taste buds might be if green tea was served in a red teacup!

But I wonder what these visual cues meant to my grandmother beyond matching her expectations of taste. At the first sip, every time, she would declare, "*Aww, so good, this tea!*" (ああ、お茶が美味しい.) She expressed deep appreciation with her beautiful voice and smile, as if she had never tasted such good tea before. Really, though, she was expressing gratitude for being alive, for being able to wake up every morning and enjoy an ordinary cup of *sencha*. For her, the stain-free teacup was like a clear window that opened to the colours of nature.

I am fortunate that my grandmother exposed me to this true spirit of tea. In my culture, there are many proverbs and superstitions about tea. We say it is good luck if a tea stalk floats upright or stands up in the tea. I fondly remember how my grandmother and I would gaze into our cups to find stalks, then exclaim when we found a "blessing." How mesmerizing and heavenly it was to watch a tiny brown tea stalk miraculously balancing upright in a freshly brewed cup! I loved that emotionally resonant, slow time, being fully present with something so simple. She and I had found the sublime in the ordinary.

Many, many years later, I was in my Vancouver kitchen making tea. The water in Vancouver was soft, like the water from Kumamoto, and unlike the hard water of Manhattan. Throughout the fifteen-year period I lived in New York, the hard water changed not only the taste but the feel of green tea. I thought of this as I mixed hot water and green powder in a coffee mug in my kitchen that day, and then a surge of self-awareness came over me. What has happened to me, to my old sensibilities? I vowed then to never lose the depth of my grandmother's ritual devotion. I will not lose this.

"Running Mother"

In junior high school in Kumamoto, my teacher recorded me in the school broadcasting room as I narrated an essay I wrote, and she submitted the recording to a local radio station. The station was holding a city-wide student essay contest. Writing was not my strongest skill, nor was conveying much emotion in my narration. I was so nervous.

My essay was titled "Running Mother," and it was about my mother, a full-time nurse and mom of two—a superwoman. My father, as a salary man on an executive track, had to be transferred to a different regional branch every three or four years within Kyushu, Japan's third-largest island. My parents arranged to have two homes so that their daughters did not have to change schools. Throughout my childhood, he lived away from our home in Kumamoto for work and came home on weekends. We had family fun days every weekend. My mom invented her own cooking methods to feed both households by freezing *everything* she cooked, from rice to miso soup to meatballs to dumplings. My father survived with an extra freezer and microwave, with her detailed, hand-written instructions and love messages. I used to bring long, thick "vegetable sticks" my mom prepared for my school lunch, which my friends at school always eyed curiously. Vegetable sticks—my mother's invention—were long strips of cucumber dipped in mayonnaise. They were a bit ahead of their time in the eighties. I was embarrassed.

"This is how you eat in the West!" she would say. "See how easy this is? Eat!" My mother was practical—and daring. My sister and I had been tricked into liking them.

My mother always wore bell bottom jeans and jean jackets. It was her uniform, and she had seven or eight different colours and shades—like pink, brown, light blue—to mix and match. She always had new jeans tailored at her favourite jeans store, and she brought the denim scraps home and upcycled them to make school bags for my sister and me, so we never had store-bought bags. I loved hearing the rhythm of the old pedal-driven sewing machine my mother used in the middle of the night, anticipating her new creation.

My mother, sister and I enrolled in ballet classes together at the Yoshigi Modern Ballet School. Our teachers Azusa, Yukari and Mayumi were not only amazing choreographers and dancers (who had once danced at Carnegie Hall!) but also kind people. I often witnessed how Yukari-sensei improvised choreography while dancing. Right before the annual ballet recital, which was always held at the civic hall, the three of us rehearsed at home with cassette tapes and costumes. My mother fully committed herself to each choreographed move, drawing out its deeper meaning.

My mother did not have a driver's licence until she was sixty, when she needed to drive her mother to a hospital for regular kidney dialysis. Her main mode of transportation for most of her life was a bicycle. She cycled everywhere: to work, shopping malls, ballet lessons, my school, restaurants.... My sister and I also had our own bikes. My hometown had a long rainy season, followed by a hot, steamy summer. Rain or shine, my sister and I would bike behind our mother, like beads on a necklace, to our destination. We could barely keep up with her. She rode so fast, and she knew all the shortcuts and detours. No matter how heavy her bicycle baskets were, she would lean forward and focus on pedalling. I focussed on watching her from behind, trying not to lose sight of her. On the way back home, we sometimes stopped to eat our favourite ramen, *keika*, usually on the spur of the moment, suddenly changing routes.

I don't remember what I wrote in my "Running Mother" essay, but I won the competition. I remember how happy and proud my mother was every time she talked about that precious essay to others. For a humble Japanese mother, an essay about her written by her daughter was blissful—living proof she was alive. Now I know how she felt. Maya's essay on our salons did that for me.

My mother died of gastric cancer in late July of 2019. During the three years between her diagnosis and her death, she never showed any worries, remaining calm and positive. She continued the Hawaiian dancing she loved, managed her neighbourhood's association as she had done for years, cared for her family and periodically sent food packages to me in Canada. She even visited me in Vancouver, cooked for Maya and me and performed a hula dance for my friends. She was a rock, even when her cancer metastasized and her symptoms became worrisome. By contrast, I was flustered and fearful, as if the cancer were my own.

But she always told me, "I won't give up. I want to be there for my family." And she kept her promise to the last possible moment.

I cried almost every day during her last three months. I communicated with her on Line, a mobile messenger app that connected me with my family in Japan. Because of the time difference, I often stayed up late at night. I was physically and mentally drained, but as intensely engaged emotionally as I have ever been. Our recorded texts still bring those feelings surging back when I read them. My mother used lots of emojis. "Don't worry!" was usually followed by smiling faces, musical notes, a heart, a peace sign, a rabbit, some sheep, a duck, a green leaf, grapes, a peach, two pineapples, a peacock, mushrooms, roses, girls with heart signs, a mountain, a map of Japan... all this in a single entry. I would simultaneously weep and laugh.

Many friends sent me warm, supportive messages after her death, and they elevated my spirits. My dear friend Synn Kune Loh, a Vancouver artist, emailed me a few days after my mother's passing. A veteran of the AIR Salon, he had presented multiple times on ancient Chinese history, challenging many modern understandings. In his email, he wrote:

> Sorry to hear the news of your mother's passing from
> this world. The timing is always perfect[...] . She is
> now free of suffering and living in your memory and

all the other people who have been blessed by knowing her[...] . You are stepping into the role of the elder
vacated by your mother. After the grieving is done,
your life will probably go through changes. You are
loved and respected by many people. They will come
forth to help and assist you in these coming months.

The idea of stepping into the role of the elder vacated by my mother haunted me for many months. I felt as if Synn Kune's message carried
my mother's thoughts.

As the first Christmas without her drew near, I started thinking
of making holiday greeting cards for my family and friends, though this
was not a Japanese custom during a period of mourning. I gathered stray
art materials—cream-coloured cards, Japanese calligraphy ink, watercolour brushes and an old five-colour watercolour set of Maya's, which
did not have much paint left. Using calligraphy ink, I started making
marks that resembled seasonal symbols, like pinecones, pine needles
and berries, and then coloured them with Maya's paint. Watercolours
are a forgiving medium. The black shades against the cream-coloured
paper looked graceful and, somehow, appropriate for mourning.

I was drawing many biomorphic shapes, studying all the botanical
images I could find on the internet. In the dead silence and darkness,
I was serene and happy, moving with a brush in hand. I looked at the
clock: it was 1:30 a.m. As I gazed at the blank sheet of paper before me,
I thought, *The empty sheet (and seat), waiting to be filled.*

The Danish philosopher Søren Kierkegaard says that "life can only
be understood backwards, but it must be lived forwards."[8] But when I
share memories of my mother with my uncle Tetsurou, I often feel differently. He is my mother's youngest brother, and we often talk about
her over a video call. He lives on the other side of the Pacific, one click
away on my iPhone.

My uncle is twenty years older than I am, but I've always addressed him using the *chan* ending—a Japanese term of endearment. It
is unusual in Japanese to use a familiar ending, rather than an honorific
ending, when speaking with someone older. We often talk late into the
night about episodes of my mother's life that we hold dear, as if searching for the source of her courage and dignity.

"Your mother's last moment was a sublime culmination," he once said to me over the phone. "She gave us the gift of courage."

How right he was. In her final months, her words, movements, facial expressions and even her breath were all gifts of courage for the next generations.

Moreover, my uncle and I are painting our own portrait of my mother and a portrait of each other. On video calls, we often show our works in progress, ask questions and encourage discovery. He has yet to finish his portrait of her. "I still get too emotional and cannot finish it."

These calls nurture me. When we share our memories and art, I understand my childhood, my life with my mother, *backwards*, as Kierkegaard

A spontaneous sketch of my cherished uncle, Tetsurou in 2019, capturing his timeless essence. *Tetsurou, My Uncle*, 2021

claims. But my uncle's painting of me is not finished—far from it. It is still developing, probing the unseen. Art and life interpret each other: I integrate my present identity with my imagined future, a future to be painted using the vibrant colours bequeathed by my mother's spirit. I wonder whether I will look more like my mother in the future. The thought soothes me.

CORPOREALITIES

The reconstructed scenes of my childhood in this book are not informed by oil paintings or home movies, but instead by interconnected ensembles of neurons in my brain that fire tens of thousands of "action potentials," or bursts, per second. Our perception of a coherent reality is contingent on these ensembles that simultaneously deconstruct and creatively integrate information from multiple sensory inputs. How is my memory made in the first place, and how is it retained after a half-century? While synaptic plasticity is unique and remarkable, and still mysterious, our sensory experience—sound, touch, sight, smell and taste—is undoubtedly manifested in the vast edifice of memory, both in its creation and its retrieval.

One of my earliest sensory experiences is tactile. All Japanese children learn origami, the art of paper folding, from kindergarten. Folding, whether with paper or a piece of cloth, is well ingrained in Japanese culture. In my kindergarten class, we all brought our homemade lunches to school wrapped in a square of thin fabric called *han-ka-chi*, or "handkerchief," instead of the pre-made lunch box we see in the West. I remember trying to wrap the cloth as tightly as possible to secure the lid of my anodized aluminum lunch box, which did not have a fastener. At lunch time, I loved unknotting and opening the *han-ka-chi* to see the print of my favourite anime characters or beautiful flower patterns, and then unfolding it and laying it out on the table to use as a lunch mat, as we were taught. What a sweet memory. To what else can our sensory experience give form?

I find it interesting that I am now becoming more interested in how sensory experiences affect our physical body and our mind, including helping to shape our identity. I wonder if this is partly because I lost some sensory functions from the TM and have become more adept at using the senses that are still intact. I know I have become much more patient after losing my sensory and motor functions, as if I evolved, but the change was gradual. When I first contracted TM, I dismissed the benefits of stimulating peripheral nerves and muscles to regain connections, partly because I was not patient enough to try hard and partly because I was physically too weak to pursue extra regimens. I fondly recall many wonderful conversations with Dr. Gianoutsos, a dedicated and humble Greek doctor at the Rusk Center, who had contracted pancreatic cancer himself while serving his patients. He was specialized in whole-body vibration therapy, with which he had trained Olympic athletes in the eighties. He believed that whole-body vibration would also work for spinal cord patients to stimulate the neuromuscular system, a hypothesis for which there is still little evidence. Nonetheless, I decided to participate in his experiment and saw him a few times a week. Three young doctors would brace my knees and ankles with their hands so that I could "stand" on the vibration machine without supportive devices.

After a minute of vibration, Dr. Gianoutsos would announce, "Everyone, hands off!"

Then, all the supporting hands—my lifesavers—were temporarily gone, and I found myself miraculously standing on my own for fifteen seconds or so without any support, because my muscles were contracted. I was scared as hell. I will never forget it; it was the wildest experiment I have ever participated in. But that was as corporeal as it got: my "standing" body did not exist on its own; rather, it was connected to the world through vibration. Its boundaries were permeable. Shortly after my discharge, Dr. Gianoutsos passed away. I remember his warm smiles and caring voice.

I rely on my sensory experiences as intimate and powerful vehicles that can transport me to places I have been before and those I have yet to visit. When I tap into these experiences and learn to carefully interpret them, I find myself in a continual process of discovery.

To Touch

Me: "*Osena-ka, nagashimashou-ka?*" May I wash your back? (お背中流しましょうか.)

Random woman: "*Onegai shimasu.*" Thank you very much (お願いします).

How many times have I had this exchange in my life? This was a normal everyday conversation I exchanged with family members and total strangers in *onsens* (hot springs) in Japan. Like all Japanese, my family loved to visit the many different *onsens* in my hometown, sometimes several times a week. In *onsens*, people undress and relax and bathe in the water, not only with family and friends, but also with strangers of the same gender. Japanese bathing culture dates back to the year 720 CE, and Japanese people today enjoy nearly 30,000 *onsens* throughout Japan. This is partly due to geology—some of the deep pools are products of earthquakes!

At *onsens,* there is the unspoken custom of washing the backs of nearby strangers, including elders. It might seem unimaginable to someone like my teenage daughter, who grew up in North America; the body is more of a private affair in the West. By contrast, Japanese people find it natural to touch and be touched in a non-sexual way in the context of an *onsen.* There is even a related Japanese term: *su-ki-n shi-ppu,* a made-up word that translates to "skinship," or "physical contact" or

"bonding." *Su-ki-n shi-ppu* is a result of a process called *wasei eigo* (スキ
ンシップ), which refers to words or phrases created in Japan by com-
bining English words or adopting them into the Japanese language with
a Japanese twist. Once we started washing someone's back, we often
asked politely, using the honorific form, "How is the pressure? Should I
scrub harder? Have I missed a spot?" Nearly every time, I would receive
great appreciation and an offer to reciprocate.

I don't remember when and how I was taught to follow the practice, but I do remember enjoying an outdoor *onsen* and washing my
beloved grandmother's back as early as four years old. I washed my
grandmother's and mother's backs countless times. These were precious opportunities for me to have direct, intimate physical contact with
my loved ones and express my care and gratitude. I can even recall the
feel of the water quality in my fingertips, as each *onsen* had different
dissolved impurities. I also still vividly remember the ineffable feeling of
washing my grandmother's back when she was close to ninety years old.
I wept as I observed her small, frail frame, wanting to continue gently
scrubbing her for as long as I could. Luckily, my tears were invisible in
the steamy *onsen*.

The Japanese concept *ma* (間) means the space that exists among
and between our bodies. A Japanese proverb reminds us to cherish *ma*,
both the human space and the space we share with all other beings:
sode-fureau-mo-tashou-no-en　(袖振り合うも多生の縁). This means
that even the contact of two people's sleeves was the result of fate from
a previous life. I find this Japanese quote spiritual and sensuous. Just
as within the *mitsuba* ritual that my grandmother taught me when
I was six, we Japanese are taught to combine our senses, interactions
and meanings: the moment two people's sleeves come close and briefly touch, even if unnoticed, there is *ma* between them. The sensuous
surfaces evoke and reveal our spiritual and relational nature. Because
it is hidden and discrete, I find I am even more drawn to it. *Ma* is everywhere—we just need to know how to sense it.

I lived in Tokyo for eight years. I used to commute to school
and work by subway, and I would stand inside the train with the others, packed like sardines. This proximity teaches Japanese people
to practice mindfulness and cultivate integration and bonding with
one's surroundings, rather than to feel a sense of alienation. It evokes
the sense of being "in the same boat." I fondly remember many varia-

tions of Japanese *politesse* in my subway rides. Far from being gropers, many gentlemen quietly strived to create a kind of scaffolding around me, protecting me from being buffeted by sudden stops and accelerations. The kindness of strangers. Most salary men knew how to precisely fold and unfold a newspaper within the width of the shoulders, like origami, when reading during the ride to conserve the shared space. Most people closed their eyes if they had to face each other in the packed train, creating a mental private space. The white gloves worn by subway staff—including passenger-pushers, who pack passengers into the cars during rush hour—signifies respect by avoiding direct touch. A Tokyo subway ride is, in this way, a testing ground for body-learning—the lessons our body can teach us—because it demands conscious, close attention to the lived body, the senses, as well as the meanings we share with other people.

Where can we find such shared spaces for intercorporeality today? In our increasingly polarized and digitized culture, where can we find the tactile sensations which might give shape and depth to human connections? The screen? Hopefully not. Sitting in the fortress of my wheelchair, I am trying now to imagine a modern, Western version of the *onsen*.

To Smell

"*Fu-su-fu-su*—awwwwww, so *oishii*!" Delicious!

Every morning, I practise this small ritual. It started with my indoor cat, Pumpkin. I am mostly homebound by choice (workaholic) and design (wheelchair), so I often feel sympathy toward Pumpkin, who would have enjoyed the freedom of nature if she were not an indoor creature. One day, I asked a dear friend, Robin, to build a "catio"—a cat patio!—adjoining an outdoor terrace I rarely use, and ever since the catio arrived, I open the glass door each morning and some evenings so Pumpkin can enjoy the all-weather, semi-outdoor space.

But the catio has brought blessings not only for Pumpkin. The glass door faces an urban forest that borders the Fraser River where it gently joins the Pacific Ocean. Each time I open the south-facing glass door for Pumpkin, I am struck by the fresh, delicious air created by these tidal waters. Yes, I can taste it. I cannot help myself: "Awwww, *oishii*!" So delicious! I bring my face close to the edge of the glass door, sit straight and breathe slowly, deeply, as if I am about to consume dinner. I sometimes visualize the air flowing in slow motion as the breeze from the water sifts through the forest, absorbs tree scents, changes notes—from crisp to soft, sweet to cool, warm and earthy to floral and fruity—and enters my body.

But the deepest part of this experience is the vertiginous sense of reconnecting to childhood memories at the precise moment of inhalation. Neuroscientists suggest that smells have stronger links to memory and emotion than other senses because the olfactory nerves are so close to the brain, giving immediate access to the limbic system. Maybe. In any event, it is overwhelming to absorb those vivid, instantaneous recollections, sometimes accompanied with visual images, sometimes perfused by a vague nostalgia, just by inhaling.

Most memories associated with my ritual inhalations are from my Japanese elementary school days, which I normally don't think about. The memory enters quickly, and it feels like time travelling. I sometimes hold still, trying to capture just a little more from the happy feeling. I am sometimes taken back to a time when I am walking on the school road, searching for rain puddles; or I am picking amaryllis in the garden of my childhood home and wrapping them in newspapers to bring to school, common among school-aged children then; or I am running, gasping for air, at a demanding school marathon on a nearby mountain in the winter.

At first, I was amazed by how the air of my Vancouver neighbourhood could transport me back to a scent experienced years ago on the other side of the Pacific. The city I grew up in and the city I currently live in both have abundant nature—clean water, trees, flowers, mountains—and must share some of the same redolent molecules. It is also known that the amount of moisture in the air is a major factor in how well scent disperses and how well we can smell it. The less moisture, the less we smell. No wonder my memories of amaryllis came back so acutely, as they bloom in the early rainy season in my hometown. Similarly, temperature affects both the strength of scents and how quickly they dissipate: when the temperature drops, air and scent molecules grow denser. Colder, denser air carries more scent molecules per cubic inch, so it is no coincidence that the cool winter air brings back memories of my exhausting winter marathon. While experts agree that memories associated with smells tend to be older and more vivid, how smell works is nonetheless a personal and unique phenomenon. In my case, smelling morning or evening fresh air full of natural scents, even briefly, elevates my sense of well-being. I thank my cat, Pumpkin, for this ritual. The fun part is that I do not know which molecules will be floating by that day, or which memories or feelings they will evoke. Every day brings me new experiences.

To Hear

"Pachi-tsu!"

One day in the summer of 2020, I heard an alarmingly loud snapping sound coming from my right hip. I had been trying to reach the drain plug in the bathtub from a challenging distance. I had never heard such a sound before, but it was like the snapping sound an overstretched elastic cord makes when it ruptures. Instantly, I felt something inside my right hip. I froze in fear and focussed my total attention on my hip.

"Did you notice you only relaxed your muscles when I did deep breathing with you, but not when you were doing it on your own?" said my physiotherapist, who was examining the piriformis muscle in my right buttock, which was what I tore from overextension.

"Really? I had no idea. I thought I was releasing my muscles," I said, wondering how I could have been mistaken. I had been focussing on whole body relaxation and feeling some release of tension when I was slowly exhaling as instructed. I was in severe pain, but I was impressed with her insight. The discrepancy between my feelings and her observation got me thinking about knowing the unknowable and possible cross-modal correspondence between vocal sounds, imagination and motor responses. How come adding sound affected muscle movement?

I remembered how amused I was by Maya's voice as she broke a board during her tae kwon do lessons. When participants practise forms or break blocks, they often shout a mono-syllable, like Ya! or Ha! It's called a kiai. Vocalizing such sounds might induce quicker reaction times, more power and more precise movement. Along these lines, vocalizations such as my physiotherapist's deliberately expressive exhaling (*hunnnnnnhh*), which has no standard spelling and therefore verges on nonlanguage, might assist precision in movement when in an embodied context. It is perhaps worth remembering that vocalization and speaking are naturally multimodal, because human speech comes from a body that speaks.

We Japanese use onomatopoeia frequently when expressing our subjective, intuitive and sensitive feelings in daily language use. Japanese have over one thousand onomatopoetic sounds, which includes repetitive syllables and words. This is three times more than English. It is very common for Japanese people to use onomatopoeia to express nuance, including sounds of animals, nature, inanimate objects, feelings and movement. I wished I could have described the pain in my right buttock to the English-speaking doctor when she was asking me about my symptoms. I could not find other apt words in English to explain the sensation other than sharp and constant. But a Japanese doctor could have understood gishi-gishi (ギシギシ), kiri-kiri (キリキリ), gan-gan (ガンガン) or gusa-gusa (グサグサ).

In 2019, scientists studied the use of onomatopoeia in building knee extensor muscle strength in elderly individuals who cannot easily check their own movements during squat training. [9] The study looked at how automated feedback in the form of onomatopoeias could allow participants to self-check their movements during squatting with the aid of a smartphone or tablet. The idea was that vocalization can express differences in the movements of plural joints. The word *gu*, for example, enables Japanese people to intuitively evaluate the degree of their effort. We often use the onomatopoetic *guuu-tsu-to* (ぐうーっと) during the execution of our own body movements, especially as we stretch or lift weights.

And so, when I slowly stretched my sore hip and leg after my physiotherapist session, I said out loud, "*guuu-tsu-to.*" I was sure my muscles heard it. I gave a little smile and murmured to my muscles, "I heard you and will be more careful!"

To Taste

My grandmother used to make simple *wagashi,* traditional Kyoto confections, according to the season. My favourite was *sakura mochi,* a pretty, cherry-blossom-pink rice cake. It is an exquisite mix of flavours and textures: the soft, gummy and sweet pink rice exterior, the semi-sweet bean paste interior and the *sakura* leaf pickled in salt that wraps around the confection. They are as beautiful to look at as to eat and invoke the seasonal spirit.

Japan in fact has a Day of Japanese Confectionary: also called *Wagashi no hi,* or Wagashi Day, it is on June 16 each year. This tradition began in the eighth century following the country's smallpox epidemic. The death toll was as high as two million people. During this time, people began preparing sixteen pieces of confections and left them at a shrine of their choosing on June 16, offering prayers for smallpox prevention and good health. This custom continues, though it has been somewhat modernized. I see how some of our rituals come from our attempt to overcome tragedy.

Coincidentally, one June afternoon, my Japanese friend, Noriko, kindly brought me carefully selected pieces of Kyoto *wagashi* called *minazuki* (水無月), which was customarily eaten for good health on June 30, another beautiful Japanese ritual. Oh, the taste was so subtle. I have a well-developed palate for that Japanese semi-sweet understatement, a unique aesthetic experience. After one bite, I was overwhelmed by a surge of memories of the after-school snacks my grandmother used to make, like *yomogi dango*, a rice cake mixed with *yomohi*, Japanese mugwort. Every spring, my family made sure to harvest *yomogi*, an all-purpose herbal medicine, in nearby hills and mountains for my grandmother. It was one of my favourite springtime activities. Biting into Noriko's *minazuki*, I felt as if I was back in my grandmother's kitchen, watching her labour-hardened hands rolling the rice dough into a ball. Sometimes, she would also make tea from *yomogi*.

Expressing gratitude to Noriko for the gift, I understood the *minazuki* confection as a timeless connection to the love of mankind and a demonstration of our ability to imagine a sustainable future full of healthy individuals. Epidemics are inevitable throughout human history, and human suffering is an important—and almost necessary—factor to generate radical social reform. But these benefits are only possible through feelings of connection toward others and the ability to act on our love for humanity. I wonder what history will say of the achievements we have, or have not, accomplished throughout the COVID-19 pandemic. What introspection is required of us now?

To Move (Eldering)

During a phone conversation with my eighty-five-year-old father, at the time a laconic widower living alone in Kumamoto, he shared his simple, conscious practice: the act of smiling and bowing deeply to greet random people passing by in the neighbourhood.

As he went on, I imagined him gently bowing. "I often wonder about the mysteries of the vast universe and continue to be in awe of how frail we humans are, like insignificant bugs." After a pause, he added, "No fighting and no enemies. Never do any harm to others." Through his gentle voice, I felt his humility before the great unknown and deep feeling for the precious unity of all life. When did he become so round? Perhaps I was not paying attention to him before.

Imagining him gently bowing not only made me feel gentler, but also brought me an image of a golden ear of rice swinging in a rice field in the fall. In fact, there is a Japanese proverb about rice: "The more fruitful the ear of rice, the lower it droops" (実るほど頭を垂れる稲穂かな). As I grow older, I am searching for the meaning of *eldering*, and I am inspired by my conversation with my father and this image within the proverb. Perhaps within the process of eldering lies the verb "to move." Yes, we slow down as we age, but we still move—we simply learn to move differently. The wiser and richer my father becomes with experience, the lower he bows. And he bows with grace.

Throughout our lives, nature teaches us how to move. When I was young, my mother always reminded me to eat every grain of rice from my bowl to thank the farmers who grew the rice: "*Hito tsubu mo nokosanaide tabenasai.*" Picking a few grains left in a bowl one at a time using chopsticks was a way of expressing gratitude toward both people and nature. I remember how we had to slow down our hand movements to aim for a tiny grain using chopsticks. Within this ritual lies a beautiful, mindful reciprocity, a cycle of giving and taking between nature and humans. Perhaps bowing our head is the first step toward expressing our humility and gratitude to everything around us. Movement communicates.

MOTHER-DAUGHTER DANCE

When Maya finished ninth grade, I noticed how she was beginning to develop her independence. Looking back on my own high school days, I remember being critical of my mother. I entered my rebellious phase in my late teens. I remember that it felt hard to be around her, and I was jealous of my cousins who got along well with their mothers. I remember how irritating she was sometimes. So was I; I still painfully remember how we argued on the way to school for the final parent–teacher meeting, and I demanded that she keep her distance from me once we passed the school gate. I was not only embarrassed to be seen in conflict with her, but also wanted the argument to stop. She became even angrier.

For the most part, however, we were very close. I often crawled under her blanket and put my cold feet on her warm thighs around 2 a.m. after I finished studying. I was always well cared for in her warm nest. I fondly remember our favourite night-time snack, *mushi-pan*, or steamed bread. My mother loved making plain steamed buns and eating them with margarine in the middle of the night. She told me that her mother often made this as a snack when she was young. If I studied past midnight, I would smell the delicious aroma of yeast from the kitchen and run to see the spectacle—steam rising from the steamer—with much anticipation. I used a lot of margarine, and I loved the first juicy bite of the perfectly puffed up, hot, soft white bun. It was a blissful time for us.

When the COVID-19 pandemic traumatized the world in March 2020, I was given an unexpected gift: Maya decided to stay with me rather than adhering to the week-on, week-off schedule, our post-divorce parenting arrangement up till then. It was a miraculous chance for me to make up for lost time. Of course, Maya's coming of age amplified the waves of change, the ups and downs, the high and low tides. I was dancing with moon and sun—namely, Maya.

A spontaneous sketch of my daughter, capturing her focussed gaze and exquisite profile amidst the backdrop of the COVID pandemic. *Deep in Thought*, 2021

COUSIN CAMP

Summer 2020

"What would you like to do this summer?"

It was a more serious question than it seemed. I waited, with some anxiety, for fifteen-year-old Maya to answer. I had become increasingly concerned about whether she was experiencing enough of the adventures we associate with youth, given the pandemic's restrictions.

"I don't know..." she replied in a sombre tone.

The pandemic precluded summer camps and family trips. I wanted to protect her from the virus, but I also wanted her to stay active. Because she was getting older, I knew this might be my last chance to pass on to her the kinds of things my parents and grandparents had given to me, and maybe to do fun things together. Since my illness, I was, painfully, unable to enjoy many conventional Canadian parent-child activities with her, like camping, hiking, ice skating—things I couldn't do in a wheelchair. So, I decided to create a virtual program with, by and for youth to enable them to connect art with contemporary social issues. It was a DIY virtual summer camp.

I began co-creating the Future Leaders Through Art Program (FLAP) with five university students and graduates I hired through the Canadian government's summer job initiative. FLAP aimed to equip youth with the critical thinking and skills to address social justice and environmental issues through the creative arts. I felt as if we were flying an airplane while building it. To recruit participants, I contacted friends raising teenagers, including my friend Peter Vrooman, whom I had known for twenty-five years. He was a career diplomat and the American ambassador to Rwanda. He said that his daughter, Zarah, could join the program from Rwanda. I was elated to reconnect with him, and doubly elated at the thought of reuniting Maya and Zarah, who first met when they were toddlers. Physically stuck at home, I was eager to virtually connect with youth from places and cultures Maya and I knew little about.

Shortly after FLAP started, Pete invited Maya and me to join Cousin Camp, his own workshop in which he taught the history of the Civil Rights Movement to his kids, nieces, nephews and his mother, Sally, a retired teacher in Upstate New York. I immediately agreed! So, throughout the summer, we all gathered from around the world for an hour, twice a week, by Zoom. Pete taught us not only about the struggle for civil rights with deep insight, but also, through his demeanor, how to listen and hold a conversation. When I said something unrelated or missed the point, he expertly wove my inarticulate points together with the central ideas, while making everyone feel included, energized and respected. He did not drop anyone during the camp. And Sally was quick witted, quick limbed and surprisingly young-looking in her classic, short tennis skirt! Still a fully engaged, lifelong learner, she posed intelligent questions and maintained focus.

Pete had also been working, in his off hours, to promote the rights of people with disabilities. He told me that the Constitution of the United States does not explicitly grant equal rights to persons with disabilities (which I had not known), and that this critical gap had to be fixed. I was moved by his sense of justice and the way he led by example. Cousin Camp made Maya and me significantly more socially aware.

The spirit of both FLAP and Cousin Camp reminded me of a vital social movement in Japan. In the early seventeenth century, a group of ordinary citizens built a collaborative network of private, informal educational institutions called *terakoya* (寺子屋), which democratized education, offering it to all children, not just the privileged. Unlike the official system that taught mostly life skills, *terakoya* offered writing, reading, history and geography. The teachers included priests, tradespeople, medical doctors and many educated female teachers. The *terakoya* attendance rate reached 70 percent in the capital, Edo, at the end of the eighteenth century, contributing to high levels of literacy among ordinary people. The movement was a key factor in Japan's swift industrialization after the Meiji Restoration.

What draws me most to the *terakoya* movement is how adults exercised their freedom to educate youth as agents of change. They responded independently and flexibly to create individualized curricula suited to each child's chosen profession, in line with villagers' needs, even without prior teaching experience. Just as in my AIR Salon and the programs we participated in during that COVID-19 summer, those commoner-citizen-teachers had opened their homes for classes and handled all the administrative tasks themselves.

The *terakoya* spirit was exported in 1989 when the National Federation of UNESCO Associations in Japan launched the World Terakoya Movement (WTM). Since then, the WTM has been providing illiterate adults and out-of-school children around the world with educational opportunities. Like income inequality, children's learning gaps also widened during the pandemic. In response to this growing need, WTM classes moved outdoors and online, where students happily shared scarce resources. The WTM also initiated a Zoom program in Cambodia, which was organized and carried out by WTM's Japanese high school leaders. One teacher condensed the grade-one through grade-six curricula into a two-year program. I was inspired by how creative *terakoya* teachers developed new community-focussed strategies that allowed them to continue student learning despite the challenges of the pandemic.

Growing Up Before My Eyes

Fall 2020

"All right, so do you have any questions about this?"

I was in the hallway, overhearing fifteen-year-old Maya's calm, caring, yet struggling voice coming from her room. She was mentoring a student over Zoom.

"*Dou-dra-da-ra,*" her student replied. "*Tou-tou-tou. Pa-pa-pa-ra-ra.*"

"Ummm... okay, did you have a chance to do this exercise? I think I remember asking you to do a contraction.... You didn't finish? Do you remember what contractions are?"

Pop music flooded the student's mic.

"Are you playing mu—ah, okay. Do you remember what contractions are?" The music gets louder. "Sorry, if you are playing music ... it's a *bit* distracting for me to really keep... so... all right... Do you remember the difference between *can't* and *cannot*? Ummm...."

In the summer, Maya found a student-led organization on her Instagram and immediately signed up to be a volunteer tutor for other young students via Zoom. She is well aware of how the US education system is rooted in racial inequality; so, acting on her heightened sense of agency in the age of the pandemic and engaged in a personal fight against social injustice, she wanted to lift others up. In September, she began tutoring three grade-four students who lived in the Bronx and attended New York public schools. Each week, she was spending at least one to two hours preparing her math or English lessons and an additional six hours on Zoom with her students. That is a lot for a grade-ten student to take on in addition to her own demanding homework and

Immortalizing her spirit of independence and unwavering determination, this portrait of my daughter serves as a poignant reminder of our personal boundaries.
Determination, 2021

everything else in her life! I had suggested that she might reduce the
number of students, but she said she could not "abandon" them in the
middle of the semester. So, she persisted in teaching all three students.

Subsequently, I happily noticed from her tone of voice a growing
increase in her confidence in mentoring, and an improvement in her
time-management skills. Once in a while, I would catch her laughing
with her students during tutoring. After the sessions, she said to me
things like, "Mom, grade-four students are so cute. I had no idea!" I became impressed with her perseverance, caring and conscientiousness.

But when I overheard her voice through the closed door that
morning, I realized that she was dealing with a very defiant, high-spirited ten-year old who ignored her lessons. A sudden, strong feeling welled
up in my heart. Partly due to the pandemic restrictions, I had been given
a rare opportunity to see into her world and a new part of her was revealed to me. She was deploying every skill and resource she possessed:
analysis, planning, compassion, perspective, creativity.... I always knew
she would become fully independent, and that morning I witnessed that

independence emerge. *She is already out in the vast ocean, my little fish.*

A Japanese proverb then came to mind: "When you work in the world, expect competitors, enemies and difficulties" (男は敷居を跨げば七人の敵あり). My mother's grandmother often recited that to her and made sure home was a place of safety, love and tender care, to compensate for difficult experiences out in the world. While we often cannot solve others' problems, we can give them love and help them get a night's rest.

The proverb prompted me. I quietly disappeared, slipped away, took my in-house elevator down to the kitchen and started making crepes—a rare event. Why crepes? I don't know. I just reached for something special to offer her a safe haven while still embracing her independence.

Maya came down from her room after the session. I refrained from asking how the tutoring went, but I confess that I was on edge.

"Wow, are you making something?" she asked. "It smells good!"

"Crepes! Would you like to try some now?"

"Yes, please!"

Though I normally don't ask her about her tutoring, that day I couldn't resist. "How did your tutoring go?"

"Oh, my student tested my patience!" she said in her relaxed, humorous tone.

At that moment, she looked fully grown to me. I don't know if the crepes had affected her equilibrium, but I saw her—and my own role in her life—in a new light.

When Maya was in kindergarten, she attended Ms. Hiroko's Japanese class. Around Mother's Day, Ms. Hiroko had her students make Mother's Day cards in Japanese following some prompts. Five-year-old Maya answered those prompts, in Japanese, in touchingly messy handwriting. Here is my translation:

> *What are your mother's features?* She has black hair. Her lips are red. She always wears black pants. The tip of her nose is red and her face has some black spots. That's everything.
>
> *What is your mother's biggest talent?* What she is best at is drawing.

What do you like most about your mom? I like the pictures she draws for me.

What do you like to do with your mom? Chatting and playing.

How observant and honest kids are. Maya and I used to draw together often when she was young. I have forgotten what sort of drawings I was making back then, but I must have had a ball making anything for her. Looking at her card a decade later, I laughed aloud at this sudden insight: my biggest talent!

I picked up a sketchbook and a pencil, for I had decided to draw her portrait. This time, I was drawing for myself, to memorialize precious, fleeting moments, like my grandmother had done with her memorialized blue button. In a way, drawing Maya's portrait became my mental preparation for—and a kind of honouring of—her eventual departure. I opened myself to the complexity of the emotions I was feeling and began stroking the page with my pencil. Everything worth doing, including the difficult things, we should do with our hearts.

SWEET SIXTEEN

Spring 2021

My Maya was about to turn sixteen. I was thinking of what gift to give her and how to celebrate her coming of age. A sweet-sixteen party was a North American tradition. In traditional Japanese culture, the rite of passage from adolescence to adulthood was between the ages of twelve and sixteen, when Japanese believe youth start contributing to society. Sixteen years—it felt like the time it took to make a cup of tea. I was feeling sad and uneasy. More accurately, it was simultaneously touching and terrifying.

In the anime film *Wolf Children*, there is a poignant scene in which the mother tearfully recognizes that her son's de-nesting happens too soon. As she weeps, she laments over how young he is and how she has not yet given him all that she needs to give. That moment reduced me to tears. I was seeing myself as the mother in that film, even though Maya was still quite young when I first watched it. The film epitomizes the Japanese saying, "Meeting is only the beginning of separation" (会うは別

れの始め). I always feared the unbearable goodbye and my own reaction. As I anticipated Maya's sixteenth birthday, that mother's voice came back to me with a special gravity.

Why was I so afraid of separation, which is, after all, such a natural phenomenon? I did not feel ready for this bravest—but necessary—duty of a parent. In some sense, I felt very proud to see her blooming ahead of time, as she was keen on leaving Vancouver for another city at the young age of sixteen. I left my hometown for college when I was eighteen, inadvertently breaking my own mother's heart. But the truth is that nothing was lost. That is to say that the love and deep connection between mother and daughter only got stronger.

In contemplation of our impermanence, I sought to immortalize the beings that hold my deepest love and beauty. *The Beginning of Separation*, 2021

"Just love her," I muttered to myself, wishing for more time.

I decided to make a photo album as her gift to celebrate her essence and gradual transformation, using photos taken over the years, especially ones she had never seen or perhaps forgotten. Flipping through the photographs brought many memories back. Many years ago, on a bus in New York, an older lady suddenly came up to us and looked intensely at six-month-old Maya, snuggled in my navy-blue BabyBjörn.

"Look at her sharp eyes!" she remarked. "This girl is gonna start working soon."

What a strange thing to say to a baby! I smiled and shrugged my shoulders. The brief encounter stuck in my memory and, strangely, the prophecy came true: Maya was scouted by a well-known talent agency in a Starbucks in Hell's Kitchen just before turning four, and she modelled for the H&M catalogue and did a few TV commercials until we moved to Canada.

By the time I started VACS in 2014, I was a single mother strug-gling with a 50/50 custody agreement, which was the most difficult adjustment I ever made. Maya was only in grade four. As I was learning to manage my independence, she was also undergoing a huge adjust-ment. Thankfully, she was a fast learner. She watched my work closely and tagged along everywhere I went. Sometimes effortlessly, some-times defiantly, she got involved with everything I did: intercultural weaving, creative writing, music, forest bathing, art-science dialogue, improvisational acting, earthquake preparedness and the online youth program. She was not just *there*; she became fully engaged as a writ-er, presenter, weaver, actor, interviewer, videographer and my biggest critic! But did she enjoy all these experiences? Did she ever resent be-ing dragged along?

While most of our community programs were intergenerational, the ones that were not youth-specific often didn't attract adolescents and teens, despite our efforts. More often than not, Maya was the young-est—sometimes the only—youth in the room, which often made me feel guilty. While she sometimes pre-emptively complained, I was stuck. I had to concentrate on my work. I often wondered which was worse for Maya, attending an adult event or skipping it and risking missing a for-mative experience. Luckily, I was comforted by the many compliments Maya garnered from colleagues and program participants, who praised her grace and charm. I always wondered whether they were being polite, but as I sifted through thousands of photos, preparing her sweet-six-teen photo book, I saw, for the first time, her subtle facial expressions and body language that I was perhaps too close to before to witness. I gasped. *They were not just being polite!*

I was captivated with her spontaneous smiles and wide-open eyes, how she was leaning toward others, taking notes, laughing with them, or how she would tilt her ear as she listened to someone, or make clear eye contact. I was seeing, like the lady on the bus some sixteen years pri-or, Maya's sharp eyes, her curiosity and engagement. And I saw people's body language raptly attentive to her. I was overwhelmed to see all the warm friendships she formed, independent of my world.

"Thank you," I whispered.

RIVERS FLOW IN YOU

"Sorry, Keiko-chan, I could not take your phone call this morning; I was busy all day with doctors," my mother wrote in our Line chat. At the time, she was battling the terminal stages of gastric cancer.

"The CT scan showed lymphatic metastases in the abdominal cavity," she wrote. "There was serous fluid in the abdomen and in my lungs too. My feet are swollen and I have jaundice. The doctor advised me to move to the palliative care ward to prioritize pain control and told me I could go back home whenever my condition is stable. Don't worry, I never give up. By the time Maya arrives in Kumamoto, I'll be ready to have a great time with her!"

I could feel that she was as solid as a rock. How could she be so calm and still so full of life? I was weeping incessantly. When I had asked Maya, a responsible fifteen-year-old, whether she could fly to Japan on her own to see my mother in her last days, I was wishing I could fly with her. I wanted to hold my mother tight and ease her peaceful journey any way I could, but it was too risky for my body to take long-haul flights and to be exposed to Kumamoto's heat and humidity in July. My mother begged me not to take the risk. I was worried she might not last that long. I was praying every day that we could all live on Earth a little longer.

"Keiko-chan," she continued, "thank you for everything. You were the first granddaughter my parents could care for from birth. They always said to me when I returned from my night shift, 'Keiko-chan was quiet and such a joy to take care of!' My mother had had a tough time raising her own five children during World War II. It was survival then. So, you were the first child she could enjoy raising. You are such a loyal child. Thanks to you, I visited New York and Vancouver so many times. Now you have such a kind daughter, Maya. I have no doubt she will be the one who understands you the most, just like you are to me. All I wish now is that you and Maya are healthy and keep your happy mother-daughter bond." I had heard this many times before, but now it became the most important story of my life because she told it to me on her deathbed.

Maya arrived in Kumamoto in July 2019 for a ten-day stay. As soon as she walked into my mother's new palliative care private room, she ran to her bed and hugged her skin-and-bones body for hours, sobbing

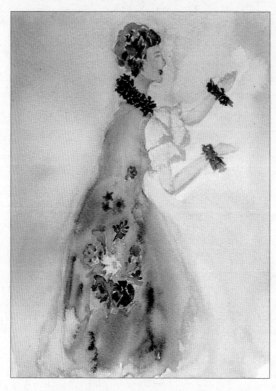

My mother's life was filled with dancing and singing, always embodying the motto "Give joy to others." I often wonder if she continues to dance in heaven. *Rivers Flow in You*, 2021

like a small child. During these ten hard days, she did not leave my mother's bedside, and my mother held her hands, stroked her hair and shared stories and songs for as long as she was able. As days went by, breathing was sometimes all she could manage.

One afternoon, the hospital staff encouraged Maya to use a piano in the communal hall. She decided to play her favourite song, Yiruma's "Rivers Flow in You." She had recently learned it specifically for my mother. My mother was carefully transferred to a wheelchair and brought out to the hall so she could listen. A few other patients came as well. Once the music started, my mother sat straight and began gently moving her head to the rhythm, never taking her eyes off Maya.

My mother was gone four days after Maya said goodbye and returned to Canada. The rivers kept flowing.

MEMENTO MORI

In the seventeenth century, European painters often left reminders of death (a skull, an hourglass, a decaying flower) in their paintings. This motif was called *memento mori* (Latin for "remember death"), and it was intended to remind the viewer that life was fleeting—that we should savour each precious moment. This is another perspective on the more cheerful, classical motifs of *nunc est bibendum* ("now it is time to drink") and *carpe diem* ("seize the day"), all of which serve to intensify our experience of a passing life.

My own life so far has been like painting in watercolour: I have had to learn how to lose control to find a sense of balance. Sometimes, it feels as gentle as cellular osmosis—water moving in and out of our cells across a thin membrane—as I've moved between places, professions, cultures, relationships, physical conditions and identities. My many unexpected accidents give birth to blooms, those cauliflower shapes that accidentally emerge in watercolour painting when uninvited pigment flows from one region to another across a too-wet surface. I have come to understand these blooms on the canvas as my personal *memento mori,* for they remind me of my own spinal cord inflammation—something advancing, something to surrender to. The first MRI scan I saw that pictured my damaged spinal cord looked like abstract art; its greyish-white flowers were vaguely visible in the dark, like a hazy moon on a spring night. It was a visual representation of my physical state at the time. The scan taught me that I had to begin making my own interpretations to see my life, my future and myself anew. This is what I think of as I watch the watercolour bleed across boundaries on canvas. *Memento mori. Carpe diem.* And I feel as though I share a kindred aqueous spirit with water. I am drawn to its soft, clear, palpable, life-giving and sustaining nature. Like water, sometimes I feel myself reaching a peaceful osmotic equilibrium; sometimes, I must flow into new channels.

One surprisingly delightful part of passing through life with watercolours has been learning to see anew. Initially, I could not see the accidental blooms I had made. I glanced at them and dismissed them as errors and disasters. But gradually, I came to see them as abstract art. *What should I do now? What can I imagine?* There is thus no such thing as a mistake. One can, by adding new colours and lines, find sense and coherence. Blooms are invitations to see anew. In this last chapter, I am offering examples of this principle, including my work in Banff in 2019, when I re-read *The Little Prince* (my favourite book), rewatched *Ikiru* (my favourite film) with my mother... all of these seemingly ephemeral moments keep returning to my consciousness like waves. And each time, I rediscover new meanings—with mixed feelings of awe, grief and love.

MY NORTH STAR: UNFOLDING SENSU

In 2019, I attended a workshop at the Banff Centre for Arts and Creativity. I had never taken an art class and was hungry for new stimulus, but I had no idea what to expect. I was asked to bring a token to represent myself—my "North Star"—to share on the first night.

The expression "North Star" was new to me, so I looked it up. It is an actual star, formally called Polaris, a bright one that points north. Metaphorically, it refers to something that orients our inner compass. There is no similar expression in Japanese. I read that the North Star was associated with the ex-slave and abolitionist Harriet Tubman, who helped run the Underground Railway, guiding escaping slaves north, always north, because north meant freedom. Sometimes, freedom meant Canada. Did I have one—a North Star?

In traditional Japanese culture, people believe that spirituality lives in all things, even in a grain of rice. Anything could be a North Star, then. The image of a *sensu* (扇子), a Japanese folding fan, entered my mind. *Could a Japanese* sensu *act as my North Star?* Fans were introduced to Japan from China around the sixth century. Smaller folding fans, *sensu*, were invented by the Japanese in the seventh century. Although they may be used as ornaments or to cool oneself, their primary purpose was to organize the thin strips of cypress wood that people used for writing then. They were essentially notepads. It amused me to think that the Japanese penchant for neatness explained this invention. But beyond being filing systems, folding fans became communication devices, and

In my experimental watercolour, I embarked without a specific subject in mind. To my surprise, the resulting artwork evoked a mixture of contentment and sadness, capturing the intricate nuances of life. *Memento mori,* 2021

they co-evolved with the introduction of paper almost 1,300 years ago. This is an incredibly long time for an object to keep its original form without becoming obsolete.

Examine the structure: it is delicate, well-engineered and withstands repeated openings and closings, yet it fits in your sleeve pocket. The structural strength comes from the pivot, where a rivet is inserted through the ends of all the ribs or sticks, creating an accordion-like support for the fan leaf. In a blend of art and science, these features have acquired metaphorical significance and given rise to some important Japanese words. The idiom "*su-e-hi-ro-ga-ri*" (末広がり) literally means "spreading out wide toward the end" and implies becoming increasingly prosperous. The fan spreads out when opened, symbolizing many possible paths in life from one unique pivot: the point of birth. Accordingly, a Japanese fan has become a desirable gift for commemorative celebrations. Another word, *kaname* (要), denotes the pivot of a fan and signifies an essential requirement, main point or key person. All Japanese children are urged by their parents and teachers, "Be the *kaname!*" They are telling them to become essential. Some parents even name children (mostly girls) this way, to remind them of their key role.

Because of these symbolic meanings, folding fans have been important to Japanese people for centuries. Military commanders have used them as signaling devices, as did monks during religious ceremonies. Painters painted on them. Craftsmen remounted them as hanging scrolls. Kabuki dancers accentuated their stylized movements with fans to symbolize wind, rain and waves. Before the fifteenth century, they were originally used only by the aristocracy, but they later became part of the fabric of everyday life for every social level, and sometimes acted as social signals. For example, placing a closed fan between yourself and someone else means you are acknowledging their superior status.

As a Japanese woman who learned tea ceremony and modern Japanese ballet, holding a fan in a certain way—closed, half-opened or fully opened—reinforces my sense of cultural identity. Beyond that, it evokes emotions associated with my life experiences. I fondly remember the time when my mom and I practised together to master how to turn the opened fan with one hand, and then, together, we danced a piece choreographed by our ballet teacher to "Kuroda-bushi," a folk song from Fukuoka, Kyusyu, my home region. The song starts very slowly, and we would hold out the open fan as if it were a large sake cup to match the song's lyrics. We solemnly raised it with both hands, arms stretched out straight. It was a slow, subtle movement similar to Noh dance, the oldest surviving form of Japanese theatre, requiring whole-body concentration. My fingertips still remember the sensation and the struggle to gracefully open it with one rapid swing of my hand. I loved dancing with my mom. We were ardent and focussed. We were the only mother-daughter pair in my ballet school.

Fans evoke hope and an aesthetic of survival within the gracefully branching trajectories of life, including my own life. So, I chose a folding fan as my North Star.

When I first walked into the huge classroom at Banff Centre, the floor-to-ceiling windows displayed a sweeping view of the mountains. The rims of thirteen bicycle wheels, without spokes, were hanging horizontally from the ceiling. All thirteen of us participating in the workshop were expected to create an art piece using one of these rims by the end of the fourth day. The piece had to tell a story about wrestling with life's challenges. The instructors allowed us to access all possible art materials, even gold. The large classroom was open as a studio for us to work in after 5 p.m. every day. I was very anxious at first, as I had never done anything like this.

I looked at the cornucopia of art materials and tools. Every possible craft material was there. Then, I remembered a friend using a circular rim as a weaving frame in our Salish weaving workshop in Vancouver. She had taught me how to warp—the first step in forming a "sheet" on the loom. I dove in and quickly became joyfully absorbed.

On day four, I presented an interactive, three-dimensional woven object, using fabrics representing various cultures and histories but a common human heritage. Fabric strips hung from rim to floor, suggesting humanity's timeline. The spiritual focus was a Japanese folding fan, representing our ability to visualize the future. The two-dimensional surface faced the viewers so they could see the circular pattern of weaving, which represented intercultural relationships. I added the word *imagine!* on a Japanese *sensu*, which I hung from the edge of the rim as a centrepiece. I attached another fan-shaped paper with the Chinese character 恕 (*jo*, meaning "compassion") written on it, decorated with a piece of wood and natural plants to remind us we are Earth's guardians. My artmaking was absorbing and revealing. I had no idea how the *sensu* found their place in my final piece, which was supposed to represent how I deal with life's challenges. I was drawn to the beauty, unfolding and evolution that fans have been presenting for millennia. My passing life is unfolding like *sensu*. It has not escaped my attention that I have chosen to let this fan unfold in the North.

MY LITTLE PRINCE MOMENTS

"I am touched, intrigued and inspired by the thoughtful presentation you recorded. It is a beautiful creation that speaks to the depth of your inquiry and capacity to connect with others. Thank you for sharing 'yourself' with us, Keiko."

So wrote Daphne, a beautiful, accomplished artist-scientist of Métis heritage whom I met at the 2021 biennial conference of the Canadian Network for Arts and Learning (CNAL). As I started reading the message on my iPhone, I couldn't stop smiling. My eyes grew moist. Was it simply the validation she gave me, or did the joy come from a sense of connecting with something larger than myself? *She sees what I see!* I thought. Why was this so powerful?

At the conference, I presented my short documentary integrating the art of origami with stories of my memories of my grandmother and Maya. The film probes deeply into the philosophy and science behind origami and its connection to memories. The story I had presented was not important in the context of the CNAL conference, whose theme was the vital role the arts play in health and society. But it was meaningful to me, as it revealed (albeit clumsily) the why and how of my current mission.

Shortly after the conference, I listened to an audio book of *The Little Prince* by Antoine de Saint-Exupéry,[10] one of my favourite books. Every time I read or listen, I experience different emotions and new revelations. This time, I was intrigued and puzzled by an exchange between the Little Prince and the snake.

The Little Prince asks the snake, "But why do you always speak in riddles?"

The snake responds with an indirect answer: "I solve them all."

Huh? I knew the snake represented death, but at first I couldn't understand what this dialogue really meant. Who is "I" really? What is the symbolism of "riddles"? Why did the snake answer the way it did?

After some thought, I arrived at my own interpretation: the Little

Prince asks the snake, "But why do you act childlike?" I took this to mean, "Why do you remain an artist as you grow up?"

The snake then answers (in accord with my interpretation), "When you face your own imminent death, you will understand everything." This explains how the snake solves riddles: there is a wisdom that arrives when one is facing death. And it explains something important in my own life. For a long time, I believed that the right path was to follow the career I had pursued for twelve years. Due to the pressure of academic competition, however, I had begun to care only about my work, productivity, status and

Flowers never fail to bring me delight and excitement. *How do I want to spend time?* 2022

basic survival, and made little time for others. I judged my worth by the number of publications in first-tier journals. Just like the different types of adults whose frivolities and weaknesses are revealed in *The Little Prince*, I had lost my inner child at some point.

After my paralysis, though, I started seeing the world through my heart. It is no coincidence that I remember almost everything that followed my near-death existence: so many challenging but beautiful moments and unforgettable friends and strangers. These are my *memento mori* treasures and wellsprings of love.

I still remember so vividly my father-in-law, Eddy, telling me, right after my discharge from the hospital, "As long as Maya has a mother, that is all that matters." Now it has taken on a deeper resonance: I am worthy because I exist. I was freed from the fear of "Publish or perish." I was overjoyed to be alive. Instead of returning to Columbia University, I commuted to a nearby playground in Hell's Kitchen with Maya, every day for two years. There I made lifetime friends. In the playground, the toddlers and children were my teachers and showed me how to be an artist. They did not see my wheelchair as a mark of something wrong, but rather thought that I had come with a cool toy. We played and bond- ed together all day, in every season. I still sometimes wonder how all those kids are doing. I thank them for sharing their world with me. What is truly valuable in life? Time. Time for each other and to live. After my paralysis, I had a different relationship with my time. It was a kind of awakening. How do I want to *spend* time?

I am continually reminded that we are all artists. Is it possible to keep our childlike sense of discovery? It is vital. How can we—even if only temporarily, for one or two hours a week—move from institutions of mer- itocracy and social control to institutions of co-creation and freedom?

The Little Prince says, "Grown-ups never understand anything by themselves, and it is tiresome for children to be always and forev- er explaining things to them." My experience with Daphne unlocked a wish I had long held, a dream of spending parts of our professional and personal lives in a "playground," a mental and social space we all long for, where we observe, interact and play—yes, even as adults! I still feel connected to her, as if she had understood the meaning of one of my rudimentary drawings, like Drawing Number One in *The Little Prince,* of a boa constrictor digesting an elephant, which most adults interpret as a picture of a hat. Daphne identified in me that childlike sense of discov- ery. This, for me, was intensely aesthetic and revelatory.

LITTLE FEARS

One night, as I was putting seven-year-old Maya to bed, she asked me timidly, "Mom, why is my right ear broken?"

At school, she was confidently open about her deaf ear with her friends, saying "Look, my left ear is working, but not this side!" punc- tuated with animated hand gestures. She was the life of the party, as her teachers often said. Until now, she had never asked me *why* it didn't work, at least not directly.

In a calm, gentle voice, I explained, "When you were one year old, you got very sick from a serious illness called pneumococcal meningitis. But you were a very lucky and strong kid; you recovered completely, like a miracle, except for in one ear. Luckily, we have two ears, so one can always compensate for the other."

I could see her face was changing, threatening to cry. Holding back tears as hard as she could, she asked me again in a trembling voice, "Was

I about to lose my hearing on both sides? What would happen if I lost my hearing on both sides?" Tears came then.

This was the first time Maya revealed her real fear to me, which I had not known. Holding her hands and maintaining eye contact, I took a deep breath and continued, "Maya, look at Mommy. As you know, more than half of my body stopped working nearly five years ago. But did I stop smiling and laughing? Not at all. I go out and meet interesting people every day, trying to contribute to making the community more alive. So, whenever you feel afraid and fearful, try to remember Mommy, okay? You will feel brave, hopefully. There are many people in the

A heartfelt tribute to my beloved mother, captured in a rendition of the photo chosen for her funeral. She was known for her radiant smiles and her love for wearing hats. Mom, I miss you dearly. *My North Star*, 2020

world who have much harder lives than Mommy but are doing amazing things. I will tell you about those people next time."

Maya stopped crying. She was intently listening to my talk, nodding her head continually, murmuring "*mmm.*" I felt a surge of joy I had never experienced before. I could contribute to Maya's life in this way! Even if this were all I could ever do, my life had meaning.

The next day, I received a hand-written note from Maya, who often wrote me "thank you" or "sorry" letters. This time, she wrote:

> Hi, mom, thank you for teling that i donnt haf to be
> skard of enithing!
> (Maya, April 15, 2012)

She expressed herself so gracefully, though she had not yet learned to spell. This note was far more significant to me than any of my diplomas.

When my mother was dying, I asked her many times, with teary eyes, "Mother, aren't you afraid?"

She always smiled and said, "Nothing to be afraid of or feel sad about. Our hearts are ONE and connected. I will always be watching over you from your left shoulder, no matter where you will be. Thank you, Keiko. I won't give up, as I want to be there for my family."

I realize now that I was mistaken in 2019 at the Banff Centre. An inanimate Japanese fan is not my North Star; my North Star is my mother.

BACK ALLEYS

My chosen route to my school in Kumamoto was not the shortest one. In the spirit of exploration and adventure, most kids I knew walked all possible routes. I still vividly remember a sense of thrill and danger in passing a doghouse adjacent to the rear of the produce store, where a huge bulldog was primed to bark and jump every time we passed. Travelling through back roads, there were endless myths and discoveries: the sap-green bonsai tree covered in moss that contrasted with a tall, faded bamboo fence like the background of a painting; the sounds and smells of cooking from opened windows; cute confessions hand-drawn in chalk on pavement; an old stone statue (*jizo*), well-dressed in a red apron and cut flowers; a dense tree canopy casting monster-shaped shadows.

There were the main streets, called *omote* (the public face), and which were uniformly upscale and polished, and then there were the back roads, *ura* (the private face). They were densely inhabited, claimed, continuously negotiated and often nurtured spaces of coexistence full of *wabi-sabi*. While over-development threatened to ruin the charm of *ura,* some everyday aesthetics in the back roads in my hometown still survive today between ultra-modern buildings. Big cities like Tokyo also have amazing *ura* roads that had become choice destinations for me. I love the contradictions of the city.

The *ura* mentality—a fascination with hidden spaces and meanings—permeates Japanese culture. With Western jackets, for example, the lining is often purely functional, simply providing comfort. In Japanese culture, by contrast, especially regarding traditional kimonos, the lining is much more than utility and materiality. It implies freedom, personal expression, movement and performative art. In the parts of kimonos that open, especially the neck, sleeves and below the knee, the lining is meant to be seen, expressing elegance and sometimes seductive intent. Kimonos should look a certain way even when lying uninhabited on the floor, as if forming the backdrop for a love affair. As such, the lining is carefully or boldly designed in colours, patterns or even intricate embroidery to express one's identity.

A long time ago, I met a famous retired geisha at her private eightieth birthday party at the Museum of Modern Art. She was known as one of the women Arthur Golden interviewed for his novel *Memoirs of a Geisha*. I loved the book, and I remember how a geisha was taught to position her forearm at a particular angle when serving tea so that a patron could steal a discreet glimpse of her bare skin through the opening of the sleeve. I remember the vivid, contrasting colours of the kimono the retired geisha was wearing at the party, and was thinking that she was still in the game.

We also have personal *omote* (outer selves) and *ura* (inner selves), and even alternate versions of ourselves. Exploring my own *ura* means percolating through my Japanese aesthetic roots to my deeper sensibilities. The richer the *ura* becomes, the more interesting the *omote*.

I think the key to identifying with and distinguishing ourselves from our interconnected communities lies in the development of *ura* that allow us freedom to express. No longer confined by academia or the market imperative, I am embracing my freedom to reinvent myself in the context of my Japanese roots. In a sense, I am repairing and re-rooting my fragmented, transplanted self. Like a natural nomad, I long for both worlds with mixed feelings of gratitude and bittersweet *saudade*—a word I must borrow from the Portuguese, referring to a mix of melancholy nostalgia and sweet longing. I have large gaps in my knowledge of my heritage—even of my family history, on both sides, beyond a hundred years. But then, art meets us where we are.

Ikiru (生きる)

Akira Kurosawa's *Ikiru* (生きる, 2015) is my favourite film. Early in the film, we learn that the protagonist, Kanji Watanabe, a model public servant, is terminally ill with stomach cancer. He is coldly treated by his son, and he falls into despair and loneliness. He wanders around the city, drinks unfamiliar alcohol and ends up at a nightclub, singing a song about how short human life is and how we should fall in love quickly. *Ah, what is my life all about?* He begins to think he must do something, no matter how small, to make a difference during his final moments. A committee of local residents has been trying to get a children's playground built in their neighbourhood. Fighting the bureaucracy, he pursues the project with all his might. Finally, on a night when snow is lightly falling, he sings that song again, while swinging on a swing in the newly completed park. I am always deeply moved by this scene, and I am vitally aware of the symbolic meaning of the playground—the effects we have on others.

The last time I saw the film was in January 2018 with my mom, as she was battling late-stage cancer. Before my parents arrived in Vancouver for a winter holiday, I rented several Japanese films for us to watch together. Some, including *Ikiru*, addressed the theme of death. I was preparing myself, knowing that her visit would be the last one. During the screening, I quietly wiped away hidden tears. It was difficult, but I felt deeply connected with her and with humanity. For me, it was a way of honouring her passage.

She also came prepared: she brought her Hawaiian dance costume and CD and performed for over thirty guests at our Christmas party. It was her last dance. I knew what the dance meant to me and to her. Immersed in the slow melody, transcendently happy, she looked courageous, beautiful. Like my grandmother, she was selfless, always working to make other people happy. Through her last dance, I felt as if she were letting us know what gladdened her heart. She was redeeming the sad brevity of existence.

My mother became more loving, more at peace, at the end. Her last words from her deathbed—"Our hearts are One"—haunted and comforted me. Her palliative care unit offered regular entertainment. A troupe of Hawaiian dance performers visited the unit in her last week of life, and she was rolled, in her bed, to the common room to watch. She had no energy left to speak by that time and could not express emotions. Her cancer had spread extensively, and we were trying to prepare to lose her at any moment. Then, when the dance started, she lifted both forearms and began moving her hands gracefully with the music. All of us, including myself (I watched through a video call on the Line app), gasped in astonishment watching her. I wept with joy; she was luminescent. She shared her last breath with me. That gift—I feel her living within me. Those transcendent moments are the point. Remember how short human life is, and that we should fall in love quickly.

Returning Salmon

Salmon spend years in the ocean before returning to the stream of their birth to spawn. Some species remain in the ocean up to ten years, while others return in as little as two years; eventually, however, they all go back to their natal streams and continue the cycle of life and death. This riverine *memento mori* elicits deep feelings of *yūgen* in me.

Around the age of fifty, I started to sense cues in my own very human migration drive and began yearning for my natal stream in an idealized version of Kumamoto from childhood. This is how this memoir was born. Like salmon, I travelled downstream to the ocean, swam with sea creatures and danced with seabirds. My ocean life was intensely dramatic, like Hokusai's *The Great Wave of Kanagawa*. I recognize that I managed to stay afloat because there was always someone there for me when I most needed it. I was lucky to meet people who had the most vital impacts on me. My lucky charm, my *mitsuba* continues to recall themes of caring, human bonds and aesthetics. Through my upbringing in Japan and my academic training, I learned that creativity arises from how we relate to others. However, during the time I was able-bodied and self-sufficient, I was not fully aware of the meaning and power of that interdependence, even though I was preaching its importance in my cancer prevention research.

Once I became wheelchair bound, it was not about "bouncing back on my own" or being able to fight. Resilience is more complex than that. Human relations became both the most important means and an end itself. Through the AIR Salon, I was consciously creating support networks for myself and others, so that we could all find fertile ground where creativity could flourish. I am gradually teaching myself that art is a way of not only expressing ourselves, but also of sharing with others—sharing something we know, and provoking others to learn.

I do not consider myself disabled in a binary sense. Someone whom I respect once told me that we are all temporarily able-bodied. To put it another way, we are all perfectly imperfect, always becoming the masters of our imperfect selves. Yet I'm always surprised when people say, "I never saw your wheelchair when I first met you. I saw you, Keiko Honda!" When I hear this, I take it as confirmation that I'm *whole and coming home*. While I used to strive to meet standards set by others, often feeling judged, the hardest battle was seeing my own self. When we understand those blooms in our life as beautiful, productive and meaningful accidents, we find important meaning. There, we can find the wellspring of creativity.

What awaits? The image of those salmon spawning in their natal streams comes to mind. Guided by water, the salmon draw energy by burning their fat, muscles and organs, giving all of this to the next generation. The streams of our individual Kumamotos are calling.

I am forever guided along an imaginary waterway,
walking its path with a sense of purpose and wonder.
Water Ways, 2022

A LETTER FROM MY DAUGHTER

ELEVEN-YEAR-OLD MAYA'S REFLECTIVE ESSAY FOLLOWING
AIR SALON 100

I've been attending the salon for as long as I can remember. Music, poetry, science, the humanities. I've been exposed to it all. I even did my own salon at one point when I was six years old. People come together to share some home-cooked food, have nice conversations and enrich themselves in the wisdom that the presenter has to offer. Every time it's someone different, with a different story, a different skill set and a different contribution to the world. The salon is like my own "creativity hub" where I meet new people with various backgrounds, stories and personalities. All of which I learn something. As I continue to attend the salon, I've come to the realization that it actually has an enormous and positive impact on me and even on the way I think and perceive the world around me.

Let's start at the beginning, where most things do start. My mom and I were walking home from what was before IGA (now Save-on-Foods), discussing the name of the exciting event happening that evening. What should it be? "The Potluck"? "The Family Fun Club"? (I'm really glad we didn't call it that.) My mom finally settled on the Artists-in-Residence Salon (now referred to as "the Salon"). The name was inspired by Gertrude Stein's salon-like gatherings, where art and food was [sic] shared over conversation and dialogue. The very first salon was Megha's "gonging bowls" (as I called them). Many kids came, many adults came. It was truly an intergenerational gathering. I don't think I was old enough to appreciate the calming, peaceful sound of those instruments, but now I reflect on that experience and feel very grateful for having that opportunity. Go through the years and we encounter dance, life stories, board games, jazz, forestry, First Nations' culture! I feel that the diversity, the

Every summer, my daughter would eagerly plunge into our pool, her favourite part being the exhilarating jump into the deep end. This moment remains a powerful reminder of an important life lesson: sometimes, we simply need to take a leap of faith and just jump!
What awaits? 2022

range of the salon has given me an "edge" that no average child would have. I was able to swim through many topics that deeply interested me and learn them through perspective, humour and heart. As I got older, less and less of my friends came, just me and the grown-ups. I got quite frustrated when this happened. Nevertheless, this one-on-one time with many inspirational people let me establish real friendships with them. It wasn't just "hi," "how are you" and all the polite stuff. I actually got to have real conversations with them that ranged widely and diversely. What's up with politics? Let's chat about the latest revelations in science. What is your family history? These salons almost became routine. Robert brings the pie, Robin brings his incredible array of teas and Lilia always comes with beautiful flowers that we showcase proudly in a vase. Even after the presentation, conversations carry on until late at night. The next morning my mom and I will always talk about the people we meet, the lessons we learned and how that salon has changed our thinking. During one salon, one of my mom's friends suggested to her that she try to acquire some federal funding. After that conversation, my mom created her own non-profit organization (VACS) and this year is the third consecutive year that VACS has received federal funding. Talk about impacts! After each and every salon, I take something new and keep it with me for the rest of my life. That's the real beauty in these salons. The passing on of knowledge, wisdom and meaning.

Now, I continue to attend the salon roughly every two weeks. Every time I learn something, every time I become a better version of myself. I will always take those experiences with me and pass them along, share them as much as I can. The salon may have helped me with my perception of the world and maybe my own intelligence, but I have noticed many other ways that the AIR Salon has transformed people. First of all, it's a safe space where people gather to socialize, learn and share stories. Whoever walks through the door is considered a friend, an ally. Everybody projects this sense of trust towards each other that I find fascinating. If you were walking on the street, you probably wouldn't start a conversation with somebody you didn't know for no apparent reason. I see friendships being born every minute here. I hope that this type of spontaneous interaction can spread and maybe become a norm in society (I doubt it). I think that without those (figurative) restraints, we would all be much nicer people.

The second "healing aspect" of the salon I've noticed is that it motivates people to learn. Every salon, there are people who have many other things they can do (their taxes, errands that would be nice to get over with, etc.), but they come here—it can take hours—by car, by bus, even by bike just to stay for a few hours and leave. *Why?* I sometimes ask myself. Why do they sacrifice so much to come here? The salon gives anybody and everybody a sense of belonging and makes people feel like they have a community (despite other struggles they might be having). That was my final conclusion after pondering over this dilemma in my mind for days. Despite what you may think, everybody needs a community where they feel safe, accepted and appreciated. It's just an element of how humans survived, by communication, collaboration and cooperation. The last thing I've noticed about the impacts of the salon is that it gives artists, activists, poets, filmmakers, musicians a chance to be heard and to share their talent, wisdom and knowledge. As we advance further in time, it's become increasingly difficult for artists to succeed and pursue their passions due to (sometimes) the government, the economy and a lack of opportunities. Although the salon does not "broadcast" on a large scale, it does have some sort of ripple effect. The message is passed on and the presenter usually gains some sort of recognition.

As I dig deep into my memories of the salon and go back to memory lane, I feel very nostalgic. I remember good times, dramatic times and even sad times. I remember the moments where my mom put me on the spot, the times I felt excruciatingly bored and the times I was too distracted by something else to listen to the dialogue being said. Sometimes, my friend Nayu would come and sleep over on the night of the AIR Salon. The next day, we had a lot of clean-up to do, but we always enjoyed baking something afterwards!

Moving forward in life, I now know that "smart," "creative" and "genius" come in different forms, ideas and skill sets. There is no single form of intelligence. There is no "standard" to determine whether someone is intelligent or not. Everyone has an amazing potential that they can explore and use. You just need to find it. Whether it's sports, art, drama, science, math, humanities, poetry or activism, we all have something to offer, big or small. I've learned that it's not the actual bi-monthly salon that creates the sense of community; it's the long-lasting connections that carry on to later accomplish many powerful things.

Ever since grade four, neurology or neuropsychology has become my lifelong dream, but it would've never stuck to me if it weren't for the salon. The outside-of-the-box thinking lets me get a glimpse into reality and allows me to dream big, since life is too short to dream small! When the inevitable drama of school kicks in, I always remember my dreams: neurology, neuroscience and neuropsychology (they all pretty much mean the same thing). I can dig back into my first memories of the salon, my first exposure to this type of interaction. I feel peace, serenity and, most importantly, gratitude. Every person on this planet has a story. I'm beyond lucky to be able to hear a few of them.

I remember when my mom did her own salon. Her presentation really made me think of what a life my mom has had and the way I was raised. Time and time again, I've learned that tragedy can strike any family at any time. But success is defined by how you react and overcome those adversities. I can say objectively (and subjectively) that my mom is one of the most resilient, optimistic and brave people I know. She took that adversity and used it to become better, discover her real passion and optimize the most out of what life gives you. That should be the definition of success (in my opinion). I see this in many other people who have presented and attended the salon. I've heard stories about illness, divorce, violence in hometowns and aspiration and struggle for a certain career. Each one of these people told their story with such passion, thought and optimism.

With deep reflection, I conclude that the salon is the reason I am where I am. The cause of my diverse knowledge and my way to connect with the adult world. The cultural salon fosters awareness, connections, open discussions and new friendships. Many people come and gather to come and share a common goal: to learn, teach and share. I am so lucky to be part of this experience and I feel blessed knowing the people I know. For my mom, friends were everything when she didn't have family. Friends were the ones who encouraged, supported and motivated my mom to keep pushing the boundaries and to never give up. The salon was a way for my mom to meet new people in a world that is isolating and polarizing itself. It was a way for her (and me) to learn people's stories and vice-versa. The outcome of the salon is outstanding and I think every community should have something like it.

I hope that the salon keeps attracting new minds as it continues through the years.

—Maya, grade six.

A delicate dance of colours: My inaugural watercolour exploration
unveiling serendipitous blooms. *Accidental Blooms*, 2019

ACKNOWLEDGEMENTS

This book would not have been possible without the generous and loyal support from the many individuals who helped to shape it. Specifically, I thank Vici Johnstone, my publisher, who has shown me deep compassion and faith. Working with Caitlin Press has greatly enriched my work. My editor, Holly Vestad, has been gently guiding me through the process of discovering my authentic voice as a writer. At once reflective and inquisitive, she asks the questions that help me distinguish personal truth from stylistic affectation. She challenges me to account for how my language will affect the reader as I move beyond my habitual ways of thinking. My growth as a writer owes a lot to her discipline, her rigorous command of syntax and her imagination. I am grateful to Caitlin Press for assigning her to me.

Many of my friends and colleagues helped me. I am hugely indebted to renowned filmmaker Daniel Conrad for his editorial help and poetic approach to organizing the sections of this book. In addition, I thank Nilofar Shidmehr, a remarkable writer and scholar, who taught me narrative writing and gave me profound insight into the editing process, and Harrison Mooney, an outstanding writer and the Vancouver Public Library's 2022 writer-in-residence, who provided valuable suggestions and edits on specific chapters. I wish to thank my friends and role models, Lesley Nan Haberman, whose love and empathy make up the heart and soul of this book, and Lilia D'Acres, who gently but passionately nurtured my literacy journey. I owe my heartfelt gratitude to those, named and unnamed, who have been my inspiration and source of my humility and strength. You know who you are.

Last but not least, I would like to thank my one and only daughter, Maya, and my family in Japan: my father, Goro Honda; my sister, Haruko Sano; and my uncle, Tetsurou Masuda, among many other relatives who believed in me and gave me unconditional love. Finally, my unbounded gratitude goes to my deceased grandparents, Konosuke and Tamiko, and my loving mother, Yoko.

My cat, Pumpkin, basking in the warmth of the sun, a cup of black coffee by my side, me knitting a scarf for a loved one. *Newfound Ikigai*, 2021

Nature teaches us that it takes years to bear fruit, and the same principle applies to our human endeavors. *Echoes of Ancestral Strokes*, 2019

NOTES

1. Laurie O'Halloran, "I've Joined My Mother's Club," *The Globe and Mail,* January 5, 2010.

2. After immigrating from Japan to the US, I quickly noticed how the two countries organized health-care systems differently: in the US, there is a personal responsibility for health, whereas in Japan, health is a social responsibility. In New York, I learned to make a copy of my medical records to carry with me as they were often misplaced within the fragmented US health-care system. When it comes to preventive health care, you are on your own. In Japan, the system reminds you of comprehensive annual checkups, health promotion workshops and in-house nurse visits, all free and made available at your workplace. Given the striking differences in the health-care systems in these two countries, I researched how relational factors such as social support and other social networks could affect our personal resilience and coping mechanisms and, ultimately, our health and well-being. Among a growing number of leading researchers emphasizing the importance of community participation, the work of Fran Baum and Ichiro Kawachi greatly inspired my thinking.

3. Rainer Maria Rilke, *Letters on Life*, trans. Ulrich Baer (New York: Vintage The Modern Library, 2006), 21.

4. Johann Wolfgang von Goethe, *The Maxims and Reflections of Goethe,* trans. Bailey Saunders (New York: The Macmillan Company, 1906). Project Gutenberg.

5. Emily Carr, *Growing Pains: The Autobiography of Emily Carr* (Toronto: Oxford University Press, 1946), 35–36.

6. Goethe.

7. Zeami Motokiyo, *Fūshikaden*, my translation (Japan: Iwanami Bunko, 1958), 103–104.

8. Søren Kierkegaard, *Søren Kierkegaards Skrifter* (Copenhagen: Kierkegaard Research Center, 1997), 18: 306.

Either/Or: A Fragment of Life, trans. David F. Swenson and Lillian Marvin Swenson, (Princeton: Princeton University Press, 1944), x.

9. Yuki Hirasawa, Takuya Ishioka, Naka Gotoda, Kosuke Hirata, Ryota Akagi, "Development of a Promotion System for Home-Based Squat Training for Elderly People," in *Human Interface and the Management of Information: Information in Intelligent Systems*, ed. Sakae Yamamoto and Hirohiko Mori, vol. 11570, Lecture Notes in Computer Science (New York: Springer Cham, 2019).

10. Antoine de Saint-Exupéry, *The Little Prince*, trans. Katherine Woods (London: Reynal and Hitchcock, 1943), 53.

Creating and sending a handmade card to my friend has brought me immense joy and allowed me to express my gratitude. *A Thank-You Card*, 2021

Mt. Aso Memories, 2021

Untitled, 2022

ABOUT THE AUTHOR

Photo Kim Bellavance

Keiko Honda is a scientist, writer, community organizer and painter. She holds a PhD in international community health from New York University, but when she suddenly contracted a rare autoimmune disease that confined her to a wheelchair for life, she had to leave her career in research at Columbia University in New York. After moving to Vancouver in 2009, Keiko started hosting artist salons, for which she was awarded the City of Vancouver's Remarkable Women award in 2014. Shortly thereafter, she founded the Vancouver Arts Colloquium Society to bridge generations and cultures through the arts and to offer members of marginalized communities in Vancouver opportunities for artistic self-discovery. She teaches the aesthetics of co-creation in the Liberal Arts and 55+ Program at Simon Fraser University. She lives in Vancouver, BC, and enjoys watercolour painting and hosting her salons.

A Symphony of Corporealities, 2021